MIX
Papier aus verantwortungsvollen Quellen
Paper from responsible sources
FSC® C105338

Matthias Boeing

Analysis of Cultural Differences and their Effects on Marketing Products in the United States of America and Germany

A Cultural Approach to Marketing using Edward T. Hall and Geert Hofstede

Anchor Academic Publishing

Boeing, Matthias: Analysis of Cultural Differences and their Effects on Marketing Products in the United States of America and Germany: A Cultural Approach to Marketing using Edward T. Hall and Geert Hofstede. Hamburg, Diplomica Verlag GmbH 2012

ISBN: 978-3-95489-036-1
Print: Anchor Academic Publishing, an Imprint of Diplomica® Verlag GmbH, Hamburg, 2012

Bibliographical Information of the German National Library:
The German National Library lists this publication in the German National Bibliography. Detailed bibliographic data can be found at: http://dnb.d-nb.de

The digital publication (eBook) of this work with the ISBN 978-3-95489-536-6 can be purchased on the general market or directly from the publisher.

Table of content:

List of Abbreviations:

MNC	multi-national-company
SRC	self-reference criterion
CET	consumer ethnocentrism
PDI	power distance index
IDV	individualism versus collectivism
MAS	masculinity versus femininity
UAI	uncertainty avoidance
LTO	long-term orientation
p-time	polychronic time concept
m-time	monochronic time concept
ZAW	Zentralverband der deutschen Werbewirtschaft e.V.
(n.y.)	no year
(n.v.)	no volume
(n.l.)	no location

List of Tables and Figures:

1. Introduction

1.1. Problem description

"Companies that do not adapt to the new global realities will become victims of those that do."[1]

In this quote Theodor Levitt, a former professor at the Harvard Business School, makes clear that companies all over the world have had to face a process which has changed the way they do business in many ways. This process, called globalisation, carries advantages as well as disadvantages, not only for the business world but also for nearly every person in the world. The importance of facing globalisation has always been there, but it has increased with the evolving stages of globalisation. Ever since this process started companies have tried to use the advantages of globalisation while at the same time dealing with the disadvantages. For marketers in particular, this process seems to offer a lot of potential for exploring new markets and customers. However, the questions determining the success or failure of a marketing campaign are more complex than in domestic marketing. Accordingly, the terms international and global marketing are strongly connected to globalisation and have become a key factor for the success of companies. Corporations that want to belong to these successful multi-national companies (MNC) or global players certainly have to deal with the different issues that come along with marketing products in other countries. These can have a significant impact on international operations, but also on the overall performance of a company.

Since a company's approach to these issues determines the success or failure of marketing a product abroad, these situations have to be addressed at an early stage. Among others, cultural differences are one of the major obstacles that have to be addressed when marketing products internationally. Every culture has its own individual values, behaviours, way of thinking, lifestyle and languages which make it unique. Accordingly, companies have the possibilities of dealing with this process in two different ways. In the first, standardisation, an identical marketing

[1] Levitt, T. (1983), p. 11.

plan is used across different cultures while in the second, adaptation, appropriate adjustments are made to the special cultural environment of the target market. For a marketer it is therefore important to be aware of these differences and to use the right tools to market products successfully in multiple, varied cultural environments.

1.2. Objectives and scope of work

This study aims at analysing cultural differences and their effect on marketing products internationally. The United States of America and Germany are used to exemplify this issue. Today's science provides numerous approaches to making cultural differences visible and tangible. All of these solutions and dimensions give companies, and people in general, a guide to becoming aware of and understand differences and how to cope with them appropriately.

Trompenaars, a famous consultant for intercultural communication, uses the allegory of a fish and its habitat, water, to explain the characteristics of culture: "A fish only discovers its need for water when it is no longer in it."[2] Accordingly, culture can be seen as the substance that surrounds a human being and makes him unable to distinguish between different and normal. Therefore, this study uses the cultural theories of Edward T. Hall and Geert Hofstede, who both developed approaches to cultural differences by using either a four- or five-dimensions model. These cultural dimensions will be applied to the special circumstances and conditions which a marketer has to deal with in the United States and Germany and thus draws connections between those two different fields of science.

As already mentioned in section 1.1, cultural differences play an important role in today's international marketing. It is therefore important to examine if and how cultural differences, according to Hall and Hofstede, affect parts of the marketing mix for companies selling products in the United States as well as in Germany. The following questions can help to identify the necessary steps: What cultural differences, in both the United States and in Germany, could have an impact on marketing the products of companies selling in those countries? What impact do cultural differences have on parts of the marketing mix? Which adaptions should

[2] Trompenaars, F., Hampden-Turner, C. (1995).

marketers make to their marketing mix due to the cultural differences? Is standardisation a successful method in both international markets? The answers should help the marketer make the right choice between adapting products to local circumstances or selling and marketing the same product all around the world. This study will attempt to answer these questions by applying the above-mentioned cultural theories, and will provide suggestions for how companies from the USA or Germany should conceive parts of their marketing mix. It will further provide examples of culture – related marketing efforts.

2. Theoretical Fundamentals of Cultures

2.1. Origin of culture and definition of different terms

Throughout history scientists from different academic backgrounds have tried to define what culture in general means. To be able to successfully analyse cultural differences in international marketing it is important to familiarise oneself with a broad variety of these definitions.

According to the Oxford Dictionary the word culture derives from the Latin word colere, which in translation means to tend, or to cultivate. From this very early stage the word developed into cultura, which is the Latin for growing and cultivation. It further made its transition into French and Middle English. From the early 16th century its meaning was transformed into cultivation of the soil and from there to the cultivation of the mind, faculties and manners. The term's first appearance in an academic environment as we know it today dates back to the early 19th century.[3] Especially in western languages, "culture commonly means 'civilisation' or the 'refinement of the mind' and in particular the results of such refinement such as education, art and literature."[4]

The early 19th century also marks the starting point for attempts to define the term culture. Since then a broad variety of definitions has been drawn up. The American anthropologists Alfred Louis Kroeber and Clyde Kluckhohn assembled a list

[3] Cf. Oxford Dictionary (n.y.), http://oxforddictionaries.com/definition/culture?q=Culture, accessed 04.04.2012.

[4] Hofstede, G. (2003), p. 5.

of 164 definitions.[5] The fact that they were able to collect this relatively high number emphasises that there is no single right definition. It rather depends on which field of science the author originates from. Sociologists have defined culture differently from "cultural anthropologists"[6] like Hofstede or Trompenaars. However, the general idea is in many cases similar.

One of the earliest definitions of culture comes from Christopher Dawson, an important British Catholic historian in the 20th century. In his definition culture "is a common way of life – a particular adjustment of man to his natural surroundings and his economic needs."[7] It implies culture as a common situation, one shared by more than one person. This aspect has significant connections to more modern definitions, like the one provided by Hofstede for instance, who argues that "culture (…) is always a collective phenomenon, because it is at least partly shared with people who live or lived within the same social environment."[8] He further defines culture as the "collective programming of the mind distinguishing the members of one group or category of people from others"[9] and additionally, "the unwritten rules of the social game."[10] He also intensified his focus on the differences that allow one to distinguish groups of people from other groups.

A similar definition provides more information about what these different groups share with each other and make them unique: "The shared set of learned beliefs, values, assumptions, attitudes, and behaviors that differentiates a particular group of people from others."[11] According to Hall, culture "is not innate, but learned."[12] This fact is underlined by the previous definitions and also by the fact that this process "derives from one's social environment, not from one's genes."[13] Accordingly, the group which a human being grows up in teaches him their own beliefs and values. According to Trompenaars "culture is [also] the way in which a group of people solves problems and reconciles dilemmas."[14] Thus, culture also gives solutions to problems that occur during the interaction of different groups of people.

---

[5] Cf. Kroeber, A.L, Kluckhohn, C. (1952).
[6] Hofstede, G. (2003), p.5.
[7] Kroeber, A.L, Kluckhohn, C. (1952) p. 105.
[8] Hofstede, G. (2003), p. 5.
[9] Itim International (n.y.), http://geert-hofstede.com/national-culture.html, accessed 04.04.2012.
[10] Hofstede, G. http://www.geerthofstede.eu/culture.aspx, accessed 04.04.2012.
[11] Wederspahn, G. (2000), p. 19.
[12] Hall, E. (1976), p. 16.
[13] Hofstede, G. (2003), p. 5.
[14] Trompenaars, F., Hampden-Turner, C. (1995), p. 6.

These relatively modern definitions of culture are different, but they all share the same general idea and are dependent on each other. They illustrate that one has to focus one's attention on the specificities of groups: their individual beliefs, values, assumptions, attitudes, behaviours, and their interaction with as well as dissociation of other groups. Since there is no single right definition of culture, the overall concept used in this study assimilates the similar components and the general idea in order to have a comprehensive concept for the entire analysis.

2.2. General overview of cultural theories

There are many approaches to visualising cultural differences. The main scientists that have to be mentioned regarding these cultural theories are Edward T. Hall, Geert Hofstede and Fons Trompenaars.

Apart from his four dimensions model, which will be one of the theories focused on in this study, Hall also developed the iceberg model (see figure 1).

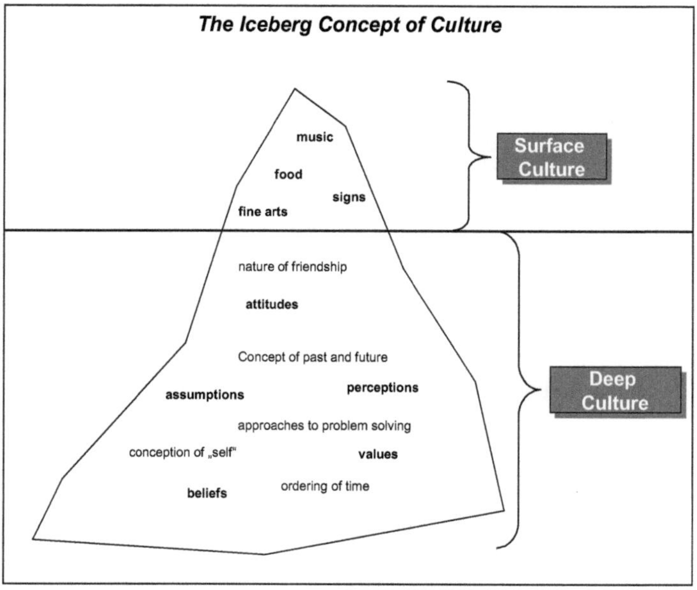

Figure: 1 The Iceberg Concept of Culture (source: Wederspahn, G., p. 35)

This model describes culture as a concept consisting of two different parts. There are parts that are visible over the surface, which are ways of living, laws and customs or institutions (music, food, signs, fine arts). Then there are components that cannot be seen at first, for example certain values, norms, assumptions or attitudes.[15]

Another important method to identify cultural differences is provided by Hofstede. Apart from his five dimensions model, which will be the second key component of this analysis, he designed the so-called onion model. He uses the different layers of an onion to describe the concept of culture, starting from the superficial (outer layers) to the key values and factors of a culture (inner layers). According to Hofstede, understanding the concept of a culture means that you have to analyse all these layers, which are represented by symbols, heroes, rituals, values and basic assumptions.[16]

Fons Trompenaars introduced his seven dimensions model in 1993. He focuses his work on the "ways in which human beings deal with each other"[17] as well as their relationship to time and the environment. He also worked on a similar theory of different cultural layers by "describing culture as consisting of three layers: the outer layer of artefacts and products, the middle layer of norms and values, and basics assumptions at the core."[18] These four cultural theories provide a good basis for analysing cultural differences. However, this paper focuses on the four dimensions model of Edward T. Hall as well as on the five dimensions model of Professor Geert Hofstede because together they cover a broad area of different patterns. Although Hall developed his cross-cultural communication theory some decades ago it is still used by scientists for studies from different subjects, for example marketing, but also in business negotiations.[19] Hofstede's research remains adequate due to its elaborate concept. He investigated several different nations; his might be the most wide-ranging research on this topic. His model also supports the formulation of hypotheses in terms of cross-cultural research.[20] Trompenaars' model shows similarities to Hofstede's in many aspects and is therefore not considered in this study.

---

[15] Cf. Centre for Intercultural Learning (n.y.), http://www.international.gc.ca/cfsi-icse/cil-cai/magazine/v02n01/doc3-eng.pdf, accessed 06.07.2012.
[16] Cf. Hofstede, G. (2003), p. 9.
[17] Trompenaars, F. (1995), p. 8.
[18] Sela-Sheffy, R., Shlesinger, M. (2011), p. 194.
[19] Cf. Bradley, F. (2002), Cateora, P.R, Graham, J.L. (2002), Hall, E.T., Hall, M. (1990).
[20] Cf. Soares, A.M, Farhangmehr, M., Shoham, A. (2007), p. 280.

2.3. Culture-related barriers to marketing

"Culture is more often a source of conflict than of synergy. Cultural differences are a nuisance at best and often a disaster."[21] This quote from an interview Professor Geert Hofstede gave to the Centre of Intercultural Learning in Canada underlines the fact that culture tends to have a more negative impact on international business than to create a potential for synergies, and hence it significantly influences the international marketing efforts of MNCs. However, he further argues that approaching this issue in the right way leads to success.[22]

Nonetheless, a lot of companies' international marketing efforts fail, although the risks of cultural differences are well known. The most important issues and barriers that arise when marketing products across cultures are the so-called self-reference criterion (SRC) and consumer ethnocentrism (CET). The SRC, introduced by James Lee in 1966, is "the unconscious reference to one's own cultural values."[23] Due to the SRC, marketers are not able to recognise different cultural patterns than their own. They automatically project their cultural characteristics onto the foreign culture: "they use their own set of values as their reference point."[24] As a result they cannot achieve the step of actually becoming aware of cultural differences. These companies expect to find the same market conditions in a foreign market as in their domestic business, so they sell and promote products in both markets identically without applying any adaptions to their marketing mix.

Consumer ethnocentrism is another key barrier that explains why international marketing efforts have a high tendency to fail. It derives from the more sociologically orientated term of ethnocentrism introduced by Sumner in 1906. According to him ethnocentrism is "the view of things in which one's own group is the center of everything, and all others are scaled and rated with reference to it. (...) Each group nourishes its own pride and vanity, boasts itself superior, exalts its own divinities and looks with contempt on outsiders."[25] On the basis of this definition

---

[21] Hofstede,G. (2011), http://www.international.gc.ca/cfsi-icse/cil-cai/magazine/v02n03/1-3-eng.asp, accessed 07.04.2012.
[22] Cf. Hofstede, G. (2011), http://www.international.gc.ca/cfsi-icse/cil-cai/magazine/v02n03/1-3-eng.asp, accessed 07.04.2012.
[23] Lee, J.A. (1966), p. 106.
[24] Shankarmahesh, M. (2006), p. 149.
[25] Sumner, G.A. (1906), p. 13.

Terence A. Shimp and Subhash Sharma developed the theory of CET. This concept connects the theoretical aspects of Sumner's definition of ethnocentrism with the behaviour of consumers. CER "represents the beliefs held by (American) consumers about the appropriateness, indeed morality, of purchasing foreign made products."[26] They argue that these consumers do not purchase products from abroad because they do not want to harm their own economy as well as behave unpatriotically.[27] Although this concept was mainly developed for American consumers, or consumers in general, it can also be applied to cultures since it "gives the individual a sense of identity, feelings of belongingness, and (...) what purchase behavior is acceptable or unacceptable to the ingroup."[28] This aspect shows similarities to the definition of culture mentioned in section 2.1.

As a conclusion, the first step marketers have to take is to become aware of the SCR and the CER to successfully market products abroad. This step is essential to effectively adapting the marketing mix to cultural differences or to identifying standardisations possibilities and has to be included in the marketing plan of companies selling products abroad.

3. Cultural Theories as a Tool to Visualise Cultural Differences

3.1. Use of models and dimensions in intercultural studies

Cultural differences have always been an issue. But the importance of becoming aware of these differences has increased in step with the advancing interconnectedness of the world, called globalisation. The first step to make the public familiar with culture is to help it visualise and give it tools to actually become aware of cultural differences. Scientists have therefore developed different tools and methods to visualise these differences.

Throughout the different groups of scientists and the decades, all approaches to cultural differences show similar components and structures. Hall's four "distin-

---

[26] Shimp, A, Sharma, S. (1987), p. 280.
[27] Cf. Shimp, A, Sharma, S. (1987), p. 280.
[28] Shimp, A, Sharma, S. (1987), p. 280.

guishing features"[29], Hofstede's five dimensions, or Trompenaars' seven dimensions model – all use the concept of models and dimensions to make cultural differences visible. Thus, it can be assumed that these concepts have been proven to be appropriate to analyse culture differences.

Models have been used in several different disciplines to enable scientists to better understand and handle highly complex situations.[30] Accordingly models do not represent the entire system but show only abstractions.[31] To understand the concept of culture with its complexity and different patterns, the use of models is an appropriate approach to make culture comprehensible. As with the definition of culture, defining the term dimension also depends on the field a researcher comes from. There are several different definitions, for example in terms of mathematical or physical approaches. Usually dimensions are used to measure lengths, breadths, depths, or heights.[32] In contrast to this usual usage physical approaches describe dimensions as "a physical property, such as mass, length, time, or a combination thereof, regarded as a fundamental measure or as one of a set of fundamental measures of a physical quantity."[33] To apply a concept of dimensions to cultural issues a general approach is more appropriate. Therefore, dimensions in general can be defined as an independent feature to describe a system. This feature connects allegories to the system to make it measureable and predictable.[34]

These definitions, as well as the explicit wording, show similarities to the above-mentioned cultural theories. Connecting the two descriptions of dimension further underlines the applicability of dimensions in cultural sciences. Hence, it is appropriate that cultural scientists like Hall, Hofstede and Trompenaars used this concept to make cultural differences visible and give members of cultures a way to realise "the idea of situated difference, (…) difference in relation to something local, embodied, and significant."[35] Thus, dimensions are a tool for groups of people to understand the characteristics of different cultures and help them to scale and

[29] Frericks, R. (n.y.), http://lehrerfortbildung-bw.de/bs/bsa/bgym/kompcult/culpat/hall.htm, accessed 17.04.2012.
[30] Cf. Hall, E. (1976), p. 13.
[31] Hall, E. (1967) p. 14.
[32] Cf. Oxford Dictionary, http://oxforddictionaries.com/definition/dimension?q=dimensions, accessed 17.04.2012.
[33] The American Heritage Dictionary of the English Language (2003), http://www.thefreedictionary.com/dimension, accessed 17.04.2012.
[34] Cf. Maurer, H. http://www.mahag.com/allg/dimens.php, accessed 17.04.2012.
[35] Appadurai, A. (2003), p. 12.

experience their culture in relation to other cultures.[36] However, one has to keep in mind that everybody experiences these differences individually[37] so these cultural dimensions are to a certain degree personal interpretations and not universally applicable.

3.2. Hall's cross-cultural communication model

3.2.1. Scope of Hall's model

For Hall culture is especially characterised by communication between two different groups of people, so he focused his work on intercultural communication problems. Due to invisible cultural differences, communication between two different cultures is far more challenging than within the same culture.[38] To understand the difficulties in intercultural communication one first has to understand the overall concept of communication and its specificities in a cross-cultural environment.

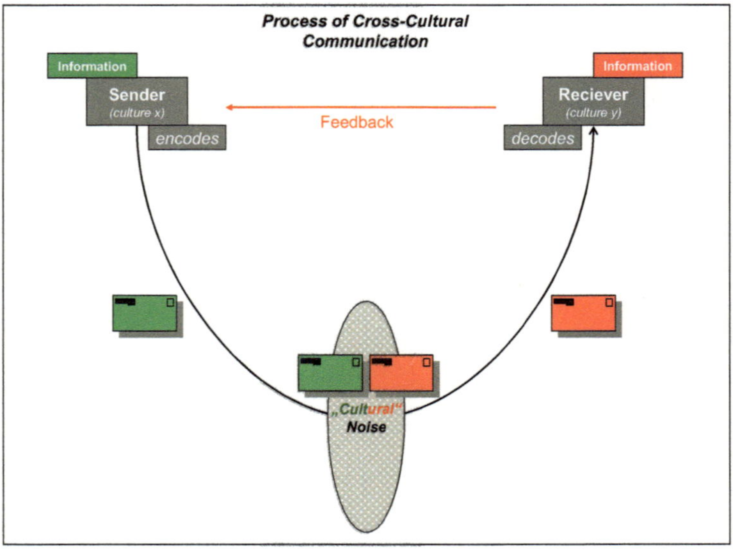

Figure 2: Process of Cross-Cultural Communication (source: Wederspahn, G. (2000), p. 47).

[36] Cf. Hofstede, G. (2003), p. 14.
[37] Cf. Hall, E. (1976), p. xiii.
[38] Cf. Wederspahn, G. (2000), p. 46.

For effective two-way intra as well as intercultural communication, there has to be a sender and a receiver, who provides a feedback.[39] Usually, the sender encodes the message and sends it via a channel to the receiver, who is able to decode it because they share the same cultural background.[40] However, the problem in cross-cultural communication occurs between the step of encoding and decoding the message. As one can see from figure 2, the message is sent through a filter of the different elements by which culture is defined, here referred to as cultural noise. Noise in cross-cultural communication is described as "impediments to communication that occur when people from different cultures interact."[41] Thus, "both the encoding and decoding are done in reference to one's own culture."[42] These verbal or non-verbal messages are misunderstood because two different cultures are communicating. Thus, in the example in figure 2 the actual meaning of the message turns from green to red.

This can be caused on a superficial basis by language barriers, but to a greater degree by the different cultural backgrounds. This process leads to "misperceptions, misinterpretations, and misevaluations. (…) [Thus,] the greater the differences between the sender's and the receiver's cultures, the greater the chance for cross-cultural miscommunication."[43] Therefore, Edward T. Hall developed his model resulting in the dimensions of high and low context, space, time and speed of information. All of the dimensions cover parts of the above-mentioned process regarding verbal and non-verbal communication between different cultures and can be used to become aware of these differences.

3.2.2. Cross-cultural communication dimensions

3.2.2.1. Context

There are several different ways human beings communicate with each other, for example by using language, but also with gestures and facial expressions. However, according to Hall's high and low context dimension there is more to be added

[39] Cf. Xie, A., et. al. (2008), p. 3.
[40] Cf. Wederspahn, G. (2000), p. 46.
[41] O'Connell, J. (1997), p. 60.
[42] Wederspahn, G. (2000), p. 47.
[43] Adler, N.J. (2004), p. 2.

to this aspect. According to Hall, "context is the information that surrounds an event. (…) events and context – are in different proportions depending on the culture."[44] Therefore, he introduced a scale on which cultures can be compared by their use of direct or indirect communication, which could lead to cultural misunderstandings.[45] This "continuum"[46] describes cultures from high to low context characteristics. Figure 3 shows a scale of country examples according to their characteristics in communication. However, one has to keep in mind that these characteristics are cross-border; thus it is more appropriate to say that the two arrows provide indications that some cultures tend to show more elements of either high or low context.[47]

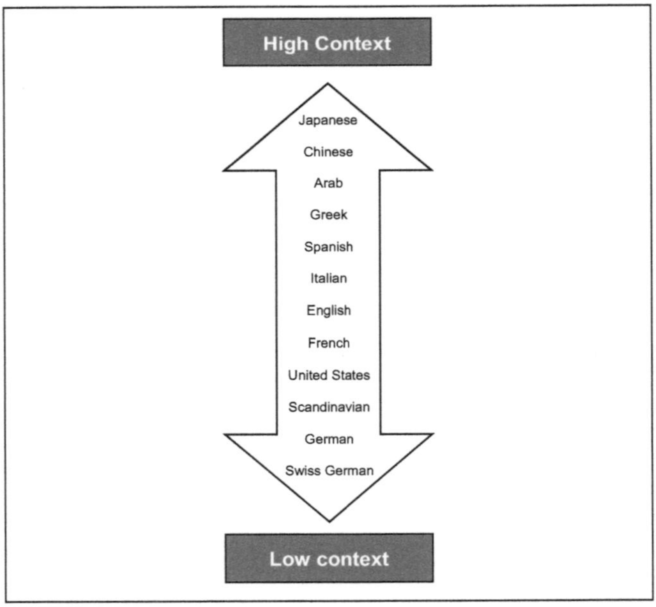

Figure 3: The context factor in cross-cultural communication (source: Ferraro, G., The Cultural Dimension of International Business).

[44] Hall, E., Hall, M. (1990), p. 6.
[45] Cf. Ford, D., Moore III, J, Milner, R. (2005), p. 101.
[46] Wederspahn, G. (2000), p. 48.
[47] Cf. Pistillo, G. (2003), http://www.immi.se/jicc/index.php/jicc/article/view/135/103and, accessed 24.04.2012.

A high-context environment tends to transport the meaning of the conversation by context.[48] Thus, "most of the information is either in the physical context or internalised in the person, while very little is in the coded, explicit, transmitted part of the message."[49] People from high-context countries "often rely on unspoken understandings, hints, social rituals, and nonverbal cues."[50] In contrast, low-context communication is defined by the fact that "the mass of the information is vested in the explicit code."[51] They do not expect others to have the same background information, thus their communication is "simple, explicit, precise, and direct."[52] In conclusion, if people from different context dimensions want to avoid communication issues, the low context population has to gain more "background data"[53] to understand people from high-context countries. In contrast, people from high-context countries have to be as precise as possible when communicating with people from countries on the lower part of the scale.

As another example, one can take the languages that are spoken in those countries. By comparing Chinese and French one can see that for Chinese people, considered as high-context, it is important to know the pronunciation to understand each other, whereas French, considered rather low-context, understand without recognising the exact pronunciation.[54] Thus, French people who want to learn or speak Chinese have to internalise the pronunciation as well as the words, whereas Chinese to a certain degree only need to learn the French words to communicate intelligibly.

3.2.2.2. Space

Hall introduced the concept of space for his cross-cultural communication process. He argues that every human being has a visible border to the outside world, namely his skin. In addition there are other frontiers that surround every human being which he refers to as personal space and territoriality.[55] Personal space as it is defined in Hall's research is a "bubble of space, which expands and contracts

[48] Cf. Wederspahn, G. (2000), p. 48.
[49] Hall, E. (1976), p. 91.
[50] Wederspahn, G. (2000), p. 48.
[51] Hall, E. (1976), p. 91.
[52] Wederspahn, G. (2000), p. 48.
[53] Hall, E. (1990), p. 7.
[54] Cf. Hall, E. (1976), p. 91-92.
[55] Cf. Hall, E., Hall, M. (1990), p.10.

depending on (…) the relationship to the people nearby, the person's emotional state, cultural background, and the activity being performed."[56] People from different cultures therefore have different feelings about whether they feel comfortable or not when people from different cultures approach. Thus, it is all about the distance between two people.[57]

Territoriality relates to feelings and distinction about and of places. People try to assign to different spaces a high degree of importance, which in different cultures can lead to misunderstandings.[58] Hall uses the example of Germany and a car, which is classified as a certain space directly connected to a single individual. Thus, intrusion by others is not accepted. The concept of territoriality is also associated with a method to show distribution of power. The size and location of offices in an office building have differing meanings in a cross-cultural world.[59]

3.2.2.3. Time

As with definitions of culture, several different systems of time exist. However, according to Hall two of them are especially important in the business world. He provides a model which categorises people according to their preference for more polychronic (p-time) or monochronic (m-time) behaviour.[60] Accordingly, "Hall examines the conscious and unconscious ways people, because of their cultural backgrounds, perceive and employ these two orientations towards time."[61] Typical characteristics of p-time cultures are people who "tend to do many things simultaneously."[62] They do not split their workday into small parts[63] and do not take schedules as absolute but rather easily adjust them.[64] Conversely, m-time cultures do only one thing at a time and are more schedule-orientated.[65] Within such cultures time is also seen as tangible, for example compared to money, which can be

[56] Hall, E., Hall, M. (1990), p.11.
[57] Cf. Hall, E., Hall, M. (1990), p. 11.
[58] Cf. Hall, E. (1981), p. 158 ff.
[59] Cf. Hall, E., Hall, M. (1990), p. 10f.
[60] Ibid, p. 13.
[61] Samovar, L., Porter, R, McDaniel, E. (2012), p. 313.
[62] de Mooij, M. (2010), p.73.
[63] Ibid. p.73.
[64] Cf. Usanier, J-C., Lee, J.A. (2009), p. 20.
[65] Ibid, p. 20.

wasted or saved. It is further seen as a way to prioritise tasks, by pointing out that someone does not have time to do something.

Table 1 provides several characteristics of p-time cultures and m-time cultures. It also emphasises that the concepts of p-time and m-time are constructed antithetically[66]; thus, it is clear that not both orientations can be used at the same time.[67]

m-time vs.	p-time
• do one thing at a time	• do many things at once
• concentrate on the job	• are committed to people and human relationships
• take time commitments seriously	• have strong tendency to build lifetime relationships
• are committed to the job	• consider time commitments an objective to achieved, if possible
• are accustomed to short-term relationships	• are highly distractible and subject to interruptions

Table 1: Characteristics of m-time vs. p-time cultures (source: Hall, E., Hall, M. (1990), Understanding Cultural Differences, p. 5).

3.2.2.4. Speed of Information

Communication can also be measured by the velocity with which somebody encodes, transmits and decodes a message. There are cultures which tend to be faster than other cultures.[68] Hall provides some examples of messages which are either slow or fast-paced (see table 2).

---

[66] Cf. Hall, E., Hall, M. (1990), p. 13ff.
[67] Cf. Hall, E. (1981), p. 152.
[68] Cf. Müller, S., Gelbrich, K. (2004), p. 369f.

fast	vs.	slow
• prose • headlines • propaganda • cartoons • TV commercials • television		• poetry • books • art • TV documentary • print • deep relationships

Table 2: Fast vs. slow messages (source: Hall, E., Hall, M. (1990), p. 5).

For example, friendship is a slow message because it takes time to discover and develop it. Cultural communication problems can occur between cultures that have a different message speed. As a result, misunderstandings occur within communication. It is further important to stress that people are often not able to realise that other cultures have a different speed of messages.[69]

3.3. Hofstede's 5 dimensions model

3.3.1. Scope of Hofstede's 5 dimensions model

Hofstede started his research during his time as a coordinator for personnel research at IBM[70], one of the largest MNCs for software development and consultancy in the world. Due to IBM's very international business Hofstede got the chance to identify differences in cultures among its subsidiaries all over the world. With the help of over 100,000 interviews[71] he tried to visualise these differences for up to 50 different countries and 3 regions.[72]

Hofstede's further developed definitions of culture differ a little from the general definitions provided in section 2.1. In comparison to organisational culture, which "is comprised of broad guidelines, which are rooted in organizational practices

[69] Cf. Emrich, Ch. (2009), p. 62.
[70] Cf. Schmidt, P. (2010), p. 5.
[71] Cf. Hofstede, G. (1980), p. 11.
[72] Cf. Itim International (n.y.), http://geert-hofstede.com/national-culture.html, accessed 23.04.2012.

learned on the job"[73], the term national culture refers to "the values that distinguished countries from each other."[74] He used this term to determine his dimensions to understand cultural differences among employees at different IBM locations and concluded that they change with employees' nationality. He argues that it is easier to collect information about nations than any other form of clustering because countries normally provide a sufficient amount of data about their population.[75] To identify cultural differences and their effect on marketing this study will use the concept of national culture as the basis of analysis.

Due to the large amount of information he could generate from his interviews, Hofstede identified the first four dimensions: power distance (PDI), individualisms versus collectivism (IDV), masculinity versus femininity (MAS) and uncertainty avoidance (UAI).[76] He further introduced a fifth dimension called long-term orientation, which was based on research efforts by the Canadian Michael H. Bond[77], who studied cultural patterns in Chinese and Eastern cultures.[78] Hofstede's concept gives countries different scores on each of his dimensions, but he insists that these figures can only be used for analysis if they are compared with other countries.[79]

3.3.2. The 5 dimensions

3.3.2.1. Power distance index

Hofstede's first dimension, called power distance index or PDI, describes the distribution of power combined with the acceptance of inequality in a society. This aspect is mutual; it is supported both by bosses and by those in inferior positions in the hierarchy.[80] Although inequality occurs in several different areas like repu-

---

[73] ITAP International (n.y.), http://itapintl.com/whoweare/news/146-organizational-culture-and-national-culture-whats-the-difference-and-why-does-it-matter-.html?lang=, accessed 23.03.2012.
[74] Itim International (n.y.), http://geert-hofstede.com/national-culture.html, accessed 23.04.2012.
[75] Cf. Hofstede, G. (2003), p. 12.
[76] Cf. Itim International (n.y.), http://geert-hofstede.com/national-culture.html, accessed 26.04.2012.
[77] Cf. Bond, M.H. (1988), p. 1009–1015.
[78] Cf. Hofstede, G (2003), p. 12.
[79] Cf. Hofstede, G. (n.y.) http://www.geerthofstede.nl/dimensions-of-national-cultures, accessed 24.04.2012.
[80] Cf. Hofstede, G. (n.y.), http://www.geerthofstede.nl/dimensions-of-national-cultures, accessed 27.04.2012.

tation, prosperity or power, Hofstede's work derives from the relationship between a boss and subordinates in a company.[81] For example, managers in low PDI countries like Austria (see figure 5) expect

Power Distance Index		
Philippines	94	High
China	80	
Egypt	70	
United States	40	
Germany	35	
Austria	11	Low

Table 3: Power distance index (source: Cultural GPS Lite, Ipad Application, accessed 26.04.2012)

employees to actively participate in discussion. In return, these are less afraid of disagreeing with their boss, whereas managers from high PDI countries are more autocratic leaders and employees fear to disagree with them.[82] As is mentioned in section 3.3.1, Hofstede assembled scores of countries in an index in which each country scores differently. Figure 5 shows some examples of both directions. Countries that score high, e.g. the Philippines, accept inequality to a great degree, whereas countries with a low score like Austria promote equality.[83]

3.3.2.2. Individualism versus Collectivism

The dimension of IDV is built on the so-called self-concept.[84] This concept deals with the way people prefer either to take care of themselves and, at most, their closest relatives, or rather live in a collectivistic community by ministering to others and to the entire community.[85] The term collectivism also has a political connotation, but according to Hofstede this is not part of the cultural dimension. It is

[81] Cf. Hofstede, G. (1980), p. 92f.
[82] Ibid, p.118ff.
[83] Cf. Cultural GPS Lite, iPad application, accessed 27.04.2012.
[84] Hofstede, G. (1980), p. 215.
[85] Cf. Itim International (n.y.), http://geert-hofstede.com/dimensions.html, accessed 27.04.2012.

rather meant to describe the power of the group.[86] If countries in this index score relatively high, people will be more individualistic, whereas cultures with low scores will be collectivistic. Figure 6 shows some examples of scores for the countries, which were also used in the power distance index in section 3.3.2.1.

Individualism vs. Collectivism		
United States	91	Individualism
Germany	67	
Austria	55	
Philippines	32	
Egypt	25	
China	20	Collectivism

Table 4: Individualism vs. collectivism (source: Cultural GPS Ipad Application, accessed 27.04.2012).

As seen in figure 6, Austria's score lies in the middle, without any clear distinction between individualism and collectivism; so both characteristics can be found in Austria, people who endorse group behaviour and people who are individualists.[87]

This process also applies for the education of children. In individualistic countries children are educated to "think in terms of 'I'"[88], whereas collectivistic societies teach "in terms of 'we'"[89]. From tables 2 and 3 it can be deduced that there is a connection between PDI and IDV. Apart for some exceptions, these two dimensions are "negatively correlated."[90] This signifies that most collectivistic countries also depend on a system with social inequality, for example represented by the patriarch of a large family. In contrast, individualistic countries do not need anybody else for their self-concept, because they are more independent.[91]

[86] Hofstede, G. (2003), p. 50.
[87] Cf. Hofstede, G. (1980), p. 230.
[88] Hofstede, G. (2003), p. 67.
[89] Ibid. p.67.
[90] Ibid, p.54.
[91] Cf. Hofstede, G. (2003), p. 55.

3.3.2.3. Masculinity versus Femininity

A culture can have two different approaches or directions regarding the role of the sexes in society. National cultures can either have a masculinity or femininity orientation, which means that they behave in terms of one of the directions. Some behaviours are considered masculine, others feminine. In his research Hofstede determined several characteristics for both sexes in relation to the work environment. He defined male characteristics to include earnings, recognition, advancement and challenge whereas feminine behaviours include relationship to the manager, cooperation, living area and employment security. A more general approach is also introduced by Hofstede, who says that a society is more masculinity-oriented when roles within the society are clearly distributed[92], e.g. "men are supposed to be assertive, tough, and focused on material success whereas women are supposed to be more modest, tender, and concerned with the quality of life."[93] A feminine society tends to have an overlap in the classic roles of men and women, hence both share similar concerns.[94]

Just as with the IDV dimension, countries score on a scale from 0 to 100, with 0 as the most feminine and 100 as the most masculine.[95] Countries that score low on this scale share characteristics like "quality of life, serving others, striving for consents, work in order to live, small and slow are beautiful, sympathy for the unfortunate."[96] High score countries share characteristics such as "performance ambition, a need to excel, tendency to polarise, live in order to work, big and fast are beautiful, admiration for the successful achiever."[97]

---

[92] Ibid, p. 80ff.
[93] Hofstede, G. (2003), p. 82.
[94] Cf. Hofstede, G. (2003), p. 82f.
[95] Cf. Hofstede, G. (1980), p. 278.
[96] Cultural GPS Lite, iPad application, accessed 28.04.2012.
[97] Ibid, accessed 28.04.2012.

Masculinity vs. Femininity		
Austria	79	Masculinity
China	66	
Germany	66	
Philippines	64	
United States	62	
Egypt	45	Femininity

Table 5: Masculinity vs. femininity (source: Cultural GPS Lite, Ipad Application, accessed 05.02.2012).

Table 3 provides an overview of from the scores of the same six countries as before. The differences in scores emphasises the fact that the masculinity vs. femininity dimensions does not have a significant segregation between well developed and under-developed countries or between Western and Eastern countries, as does the IDV dimension.[98]

3.3.2.4. Uncertainty avoidance

Uncertainty is an issue that human beings have always had to deal with because the future is non-predictable in any sense. However, national cultures differ in their approaches to dealing with the situation of uncertainty.[99] The way in which these cultures cope with uncertainty is not only a "cultural heritage of society"[100] but is also passed on through private or public institutions like the family or the state.[101]

This uncertainty can lead to different feelings, which emerge through stress and the wish to increase predictability,[102] so in general UAI is defined as "the extent to which the members of a culture feel threatened by uncertainty or unknown situa-

[98] Cf. Hofstede, G. (2003), p. 84.
[99] Cf. Hofstede, G. (1980), p. 154.
[100] Hofstede, G. (1980), p. 154.
[101] Cf. Hofstede, G. (1980), p. 154.
[102] Cf. Hofstede, G. (2003), p. 113.

tions."[103] As usual in Hofstede's research, the UAI is based on a scale, with varying scores for 50 countries and 3 regions. The higher the score, the higher is the degree to which people have a need to avoid uncertainty through laws, rules and dogmas. Accordingly, low scoring cultures do not have a need for a highly developed system of rules and laws.[104] Due to the interaction with political institutions this dimension is strongly connected to the political history of a country and is developed over decades.[105]

Table 8 shows the scores of different countries regarding their attitude towards uncertainty. Egypt scores relatively high with a score of 80, and therefore characteristics like inner urge to work hard, acceptability of showing of emotions, need for agreement, need to avoid failure and especially the need for laws and rules can be found.

Uncertainty Avoidance		
Egypt	80	High
Austria	70	
Germany	65	
United States	48	
Philippines	44	
China	40	Low

Table 6: Uncertainty avoidance (source: Cultural GPS Lite, Ipad application, accessed 02.05.2012).

In contrast to Egypt, the Philippines have a low score of 44, indicating that people are more relaxed, have less stress, hard work is not a virtue per se, emotions are not shown, flexibility is valued and there is less need for rules.[106]

3.3.2.5. Long-term orientation

The starting point for this dimension was another study conducted by the Chinese Culture Connection and Michael Bond, who published their China Values Sur-

---

[103] Hofstede, G. (2003), p. 113.
[104] Cf. Kotabe, M., Helsen, K. (2011), p.119.
[105] Cf. Hofstede, G. (1980), p. 154.
[106] Cf. Cultural GPS Lite, iPad application, accessed 28.04.2012.

vey.[107] This research showed that Hofstede's UAI was not suitable for China as a dimension and therefore depreciated Hofstede's research work and its universal application.[108] Hofstede therefore introduced his fifth dimension, which deals with the "extent to which a society shows a pragmatic future-oriented perspective rather than a conventional historical or short-term point of view."[109] This implies that countries that score high are more long-term oriented and share common characteristics like "adaption of traditions to a modern context, respect for social and status obligations within limits, thrift, large savings quote and funds available for investments."[110] As opposed to this, countries with a short-term orientation are characterised by their "respect for traditions, respect for social and status obligations regardless of costs, social pressure to 'keep up with the Joneses' even if it means overspending, small savings quote, little money for investment or quick results expected."[111] As one can see from the different characteristics a change from short-term to long-term orientation is better in terms of economics growth since the low saving rates can have a significant negative impact on the economy of a country. This aspect is also valid in terms of the scarcity of natural resources.[112]

Long-Term Orientation		
China	116	Long-Term
Austria	31	
Germany	31	
United States	29	
Philippines	19	
Egypt	n/a	Short-Term

Table 7: Long-term orientation (source: Cultural GPS Lite, Ipad Application, accessed 02.05.2012).

According to table 6, China's score is higher than any other country, emphasising their large respect towards "perseverance and acceptance of change."[113] At the

[107] Cf. Marshall Matthews, B. p. 117.
[108] Cf. McSweeney, B. (2002), p. 106.
[109] Cultural GPS Lite, iPad Application, accessed 28.04.2012.
[110] Hofstede, G. (2003), p. 173.
[111] Ibid, p. 173.
[112] Cf. Hofstede, G. (2003), p. 173.
[113] Cultural GPS Lite iPad Application, accessed 02.05.2012.

other end, the Philippines score low because of their attitude towards "absolute truth, concern for stability and conventional/traditional [orientation]."[114]

3.4. The American and German cultures according to Hall and Hofstede

Germany and the United States of America are both low-context cultures. However, there are also differences between these two national cultures. Germans try to explain everything in great detail and particularly like to use examples and facts to state a point very explicitly. Another fact that supports Germans' highly low-context position is their language. Compared to English they have a lot of different words with the same meaning, which underlines their attitude towards the importance of words. People in the United States exaggerate a lot and often use humour to ease a conversation.[115] Generally speaking, both countries have similar characteristics of a low-context culture with rather small differences.

Both the USA and Germany are monochromic cultures and thus share the obvious characteristics mentioned in table 1. However, Germany is even more time structured and dependent on time concepts than the United States. Whereas Americans try to get results as soon as possible, Germans need to have more background information before making a decision, decelerating the decision making process compared to the United States.

Two major differences can be identified in their preferences about space and speed of messages. Germany's and the United States' attitudes towards space can be related to their geographical size. Due to the fact that the USA is considerably larger, Americans lay a greater emphasis on space and openness. This can be seen in the size of houses or cars, which are larger in the USA.

Moreover, the attitude towards privacy contributes to this dimension. Privacy is significantly more important in Germany than it is in the USA. Germans respect each other's private life by avoiding personal questions or small talks with strangers, whereas Americans are used to interacting with neighbours or engaging in general small talk. Germans try to maintain a certain distance with strangers. Even if two people in Germany have regular contact they still use the formal form

---

[114] Ibid, accessed 02.05.2012.

[115] Cf. Hall, E., Hall, M. (1990), p. 49f., p. 146.

of address and last names. In contrast to Americans, they also do not like to smile a lot to strangers, which further underlines Germans' preference for more privacy. Another important difference can be identified in their attitude towards speed of messages. Whereas Americans tend to be high speed, Germans prefer slow message speeds. This can be seen in the fact that Germans need significantly more time than Americans to make decisions or answer to a question. It also applies to friendships. It is often easier for Americans to get to know new people and to develop friendships. However, these friendships are often criticised as superficial, since it normally takes some time to get to know people for a deep relationship.[116]
Americans and Germans are both low on the PDI, with a difference of 5 in their scores. In these two national cultures inequality among people is therefore only accepted to a low degree. Especially in the United States, the concept of freedom for every citizen is strongly connected to their attitude towards inequality, enhanced by the focus on equal rights in all parts of American society. This is also emphasised by the term American Dream, which is defined as "the idea by which equality of opportunity is available to any Americans, allowing the highest aspirations and goals to be achieved."[117] In the work environments of both countries employees are expected to share their feelings and ideas with the top management. All hierarchies tend to have a direct way of communication and everybody is expected to take part in discussions.[118]
With a score of 67 on the IDV, Germany can be seen as an individualistic country, but the United States is the clear leader in this index with a score of 97, making it the most individualistic-oriented national culture among the investigated countries. Americans are more self-oriented than Germans and lay a higher focus on themselves and their closes family. However, Germany also has a strong focus on small families and self-actualisation.[119] The high score in the United States can be explained by Americans' attitude towards personal success. Americans are more likely to judge people they don't know by their personal accomplishments and achievements or their status symbols like cars, houses or place of residence. This self-oriented attitude can also lead to the fact that Americans are not able to un-

[116] Cf. Hall, E., Hall, M. (1990), p. 35ff.
[117] Oxford Dictionary (n.y.), http://oxforddictionaries.com/definition/American?q=American+dream#American__6, accessed 19.05.2012.
[118] Cf. Itim International (n.y.), http://geert-hofstede.com/united-states.html, accessed 19.05.2012.
[119] Cf. Itim International (n.y.), http://geert-hofstede.com/germany.html, accessed 19.05.2012.

derstand or even become aware of differences in more collectivistic, less individualistic countries.[120]

Germany and the United States share similar attitudes towards the roles of the sexes. They are both more masculine–oriented, following the rule "live in order to work". It is normal to show your personal success and focus on personal achievements.[121]

One very important difference between Germans and Americans can be seen in how they deal with uncertainty. Whereas Germans like to avoid uncertainty as much as possible, Americans accept it and are more open to something new, for example innovations, new products or new ideas or approaches in general. There is also no need for a lot of rules.[122] In comparison, Germans are characterised by rules and their adherence and a certain kind of aggressiveness, intolerance and security awareness.[123]

Germany and the United States have a relatively similar score on the LTO, making them both short-term oriented. This aspect is supported by the concept of this dimension, which shows a clear distinction between the Eastern countries like China and the Western world. Both Germany and the United States share characteristics like respect for traditions and focus on quick results.[124] They also show a desire to be able to keep up with other people in terms of status symbols etc.[125]

Figure 5 illustrates the general similarities and major differences between the United States and Germany. By applying Hall's as well as Hofstede's dimensions it emerges that both countries share a large amount of similar characteristics in their national cultures. Their general concept of time and context and their preference for low power distance, individualism, masculinity as well as their short-term orientation show significant similarities. Major differences can be found in their concept of space and speed of message as well as their feelings about uncertainty avoidance.

---

[120] Cf. Jandt, F. (2010) p. 165.
[121] Cf. Itim International (n.y.), http://geert-hofstede.com/germany.html, accessed 19.05.2012.
[122] Cf. Itim International (n.y.), http://geert-hofstede.com/united-states.html, accessed 19.05.2012.
[123] Cf. Jandt, F. (2010) p. 174.
[124] Cf. Hofstede, G. (2003), p. 173.
[125] Cf. Jandt, F. (2010), p. 180.

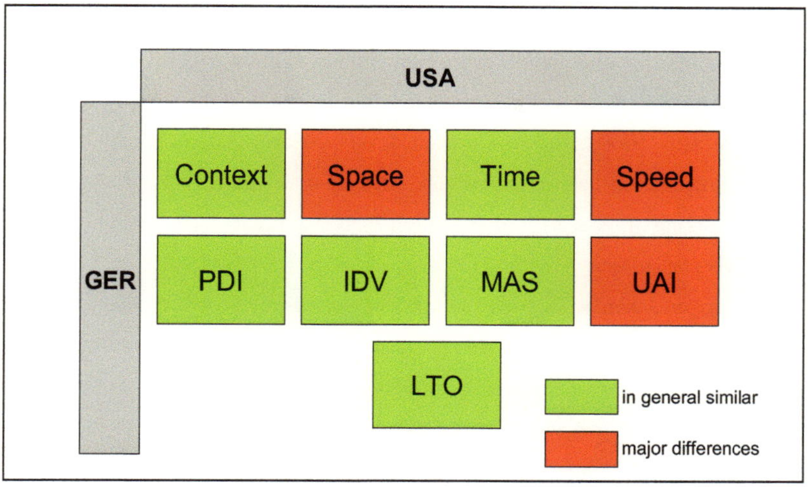

Figure 4: Similarities and differences between the USA and Germany (source: author's illustration).

3.5. Critique of the theories of Hall and Hofstede

Both models raise awareness of cultural differences. However, there are some major points of criticism that have to be mentioned. On the one hand, it is important to take into account that, particularly in highly populated countries like the United States of America, which has always been a country with high immigration rates from several different cultures, these models are generalisations of cultural patterns.[126] Regarding the definition of a model, which is provided in section 3.1, these models are only abstractions of the entire process, and so they don't take all aspects into account.[127] Especially in the USA, but also in countries with smaller populations like Germany, several different cultures collide. Thus, there are always exceptions within a country, for instance some citizens or regions that do not fit the frame.[128]

This process has the effect of diluting the origins of culture in such a way that compelling results are hard to generate. Since Hall only interviewed people from

[126] Cf. Clearly Cultural (n.y.), http://www.clearlycultural.com/geert-hofstede-cultural-dimensions, accessed 20.04.2012.
[127] Cf. Hall, E. (1976), p. 14.
[128] Cf. Clearly Cultural (n.y.), http://www.clearlycultural.com/geert-hofstede-cultural-dimensions, accessed 20.04.2012.

the western parts of Germany, excluding East and South Germany, his study does not take into account the entire population of Germany. This further underlines the issue of different cultural regions within a country. Moreover, these theories, especially Hall's work, have been developed decades ago, while the process of globalisation has reached a new stage of development by speeding up the networking of the world. Globalisation itself is a driving force behind the diluting effect on cultures.

On the other hand, Hofstede especially used interviews to generate a sufficient amount of material to build his theory. Research methods in an intercultural context can have a significantly different outcome than research methods with only one culture involved. This can also be related to the issue of cross-cultural communication defined in section 3.2.1. In particular, interviews between two different cultures can be difficult since there is a "risk (…) in that any effort to explain or understand culture related phenomena (…) may lead researchers either to make false assumptions, or to perceive difference as an oddity, both of which can misdirect the research interview, the nature of the data, and the interpretations."[129] Intercultural scientists also are at risk of being a "subject to the implicit perceptions of their own culture."[130]

Another drawback in Hofstede's work that needs to be mentioned is the scale of his research. Because he interviewed only employees from one company, there is the possibility that his subjects share a specific organisational culture distinct from their national culture, which could also lead to diluted results.[131] Hofstede also evaluated his theory in a work environment, thus his dimensions are work-related and were not originally intended to be used to reflect these findings on marketing.[132]

---

[129] Shah, S. (2004) p. 7.

[130] Hall, E., Hall, M. (1990), p. xx.

[131] Cf. McSweeney, B. (2002), p. 94f.

[132] Cf. de Mooij, M., Hofstede, G. (2010), p. 102.

4. Marketing Across Cultures

4.1. Concept of marketing abroad

4.1.1. Distinction between different geographical marketing terms

The concept of marketing in general is the effort a company spends on designing and conducting all different processes related to the product, price, promotion, place and people. These efforts, called the marketing mix, are aligned to create customer satisfaction as well as competitive advantages. Therefore, companies develop specific marketing strategies, which differ from company to company and their geographical target market.

There are five different types of marketing that can be identified based on their geographical concept: domestic marketing, export marketing, international marketing, multinational marketing and global marketing. A corporation which is only active in its country of origin implements a domestic marketing plan. This plan is shaped by the unique environment within this country in terms of domestic consumer needs, industry trends, economics, technology and politics.

In domestic marketing, companies are likely to behave ethnocentrically by ignoring changes to the international environment or competition. However, many companies have started to take competitors from outside their country into account in their domestic marketing.[133]

Between domestic and international marketing lies export marketing. This refers to international customers willing to buy products normally sold only domestically. Companies operating domestically initially meet this international demand by exporting a specific surplus of their product. If the domestic market share as well as the export market of a country do not offer further potential for growth, companies move to international marketing.[134]

International marketing has been defined in several different ways. A broad definition reads: "The performance of business activities designed to plan, price and direct the flow of a company's goods and services to consumers or users in more

[133] Cf. Kotabe, M., Helsen, K. (2009), p. 3.
[134] Cf. Kotabe, M., Helsen, K. (2009), p. 4ff.

than one nation for a profit."[135] After gaining experience in export marketing, corporations often see more potential to grow and therefore expand their customer range by doing international marketing, which is often characterised by its polycentric orientation. This aspect accounts for local cultural differences in the foreign markets which have to be addressed, so that that any marketing effort abroad has to be individually planned. That process, called adaptation, can lead to several local subsidiaries, which work almost independently of their parent company in terms of products and marketing; this will be further discussed in section 4.1.2..[136]
Another component to distinguish international marketing is provided by Cateora and Graham. They argue that international marketing can be differentiated by the fact that a company is not only selling those products abroad but also producing them in foreign factories. These are built on purpose to exclusively meet customer demand in that specific country.[137] Compared to domestic marketing, the overall aim of creating consumer satisfaction as well as competitive advantage remains similar, but international marketers of MNCs have to deal with more aspects coming from the environments they are selling their products in. These additional tasks make international marketing complex. Marketers not only have to consider the typical uncontrollable domestic parts of the environment mentioned before, but they also have to take into account additional issues in other countries, which are also uncontrollable. For example, they have to be aware of different political systems or technological standards or cultural differences.[138]
If a company actively markets its products in several countries all over the world, it starts to regionalise its marketing efforts. The products within these regions become increasingly standardised and the company also often develops similar components within the regions' marketing mix. This type of geographic marketing is called multinational marketing.[139]
The last type of geographical marketing is called global marketing. Global companies like Coca Cola Company see the world as one market without borders and segments like income. In contrast to international marketing, this process does not focus on adapting to the local environment but on standardising the products as

[135] Cateora, P.R., Graham, J.L. (2002), p. 7.
[136] Cf. Bradley, F. (2002), p. 3f.
[137] Cf. Cateora, P.R., Graham, J.L. (2002), p. 21.
[138] Ibid, p. 8f.
[139] Cf. Kotabe, M., Helsen, K. (2011), p. 17f.

much as possible and reorganising the company's structure in a global view.[140] However, it is important to remember that there is no clear distinction between the different geographical marketing types, so it is possible that companies use a mix of both standardisation and adaptation even in global marketing. The globally operating beverages supplier Coca Cola for example applies adaptation to its products in terms of special tastes in different countries.[141]
Furthermore, in a lot of the literature the different marketing terms are often mixed and not clearly distinguished. For this reason, this paper does not use a single definition of marketing across borders but includes several different areas of international as well as global marketing.

4.1.2. Standardisation vs. adaptation

For the different types of marketing explained in section 4.1.1, marketers have two different ways to conceive their marketing efforts, namely standardisation or adaptation, also called customisation.[142] Levitt especially argues for standardising marketing across the world. In his research, published in the late 20th century, he argued that the entire market had been homogenised and that therefore marketing efforts all over the world could be standardised.[143] However, his argumentation regarding the problem of adaptation versus standardisation was the starting point for a debate about whether culture has an effect on marketing and, if so, which direction is more beneficial for companies selling products abroad.[144]
A study conducted by Brei, D'Avila, Camargo and Engels in 2011 found that both approaches are necessary in international marketing, as both have advantages as well as disadvantages for a company.[145] "While standardisation applies a "product-driven orientation (…) customization is inspired by a market-driven mindset."[146] Supporters of the adaptation approach argue that markets are not identical and that the product therefore has to be adapted to the special characteristics of the

---

[140] Cf. Cateora, P.R., Graham, J.L. (2002), p. 21.
[141] Cf. Bradley, F. (2002), p. 174.
[142] Cf. Balbaaki, I.B., Malhorta, N.K. (1995).
[143] Cf. Levitt, T. (1983).
[144] Cf. Bradley, F. (2002), p.173.
[145] Cf. Brei, V., D'Avila, L., Camargo, L.F., Engels, J. (2011), p. 266–287.
[146] Kotabe, M., Helsen, K. (2011), p. 335.

each market to better supply customer needs and increase their satisfaction.[147] Researchers also argue that it is not a question of deciding for one option but to what degree the product should be adapted to local conditions.[148] To determine to which degree adaptation is necessary it is important to identify differences in the uncontrollable environment of a foreign country compared to the domestic market.

Standardisation is attractive to companies because it brings economies of scale in various areas such as production, promotion, distribution and R&D.[149] Economies of scale refers to the effect of a company's costs being lowered when it produces larger amounts of the same product because fixed costs remain constant.[150] Due to lower production costs companies can offer their products to the customer at a lower price, improving the company's position against local companies.[151] However, there is no single right answer to the question of which of these strategies are in general more beneficial, so marketers are challenged to find the right balance.[152] This also depends on the type of product and on how similar the country is to the domestic market. According to Frank Bradley, there is a connection between culture and the scale of standardisation.[153]

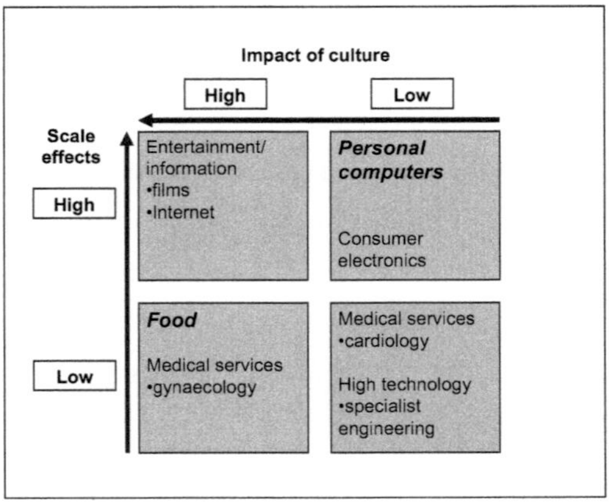

Figure 5: Relationship between culture and standardisation (source: Bradley, F., International Marketing Strategy, p. 175).

---

[147] Cf. Bradley, F. (2002), p.173.
[148] Cf. Jain, S.C. (2007), p. 4ff.
[149] Cf. Balbaaki, I.B., Malhorta, N.K. (1995) p. 182.
[150] Cf. Gabler Wirtschaftslexikon (n.y.), http://wirtschaftslexikon.gabler.de/Definition/economies-of-scale.html, accessed 05.05.2012.
[151] Cf. Kotabe, M., Helsen, K. (2011), p. 338.
[152] Cf. Ghemawat, P. (2007), p. 2.
[153] Cf. Bradley, F. (2002), p. 175.

Figure 5 shows the relations of these two topics and their importance in specific industries. The food industry for example requires high adaptions to the local culture, since the impact of culture on this industry is high whereas the scale effects of standardisation are low. Accordingly, adaptation should be found more often in companies such as fast food restaurants, like Burger King or McDonalds. In contrast, the consumer electronics industry has a high score on scale effects and a low impact of culture. Therefore, companies like Apple Inc. do not need to adapt their products, like the iPhone; they can sell a standardised version in several different countries.

4.2. Cultural differences and their effect on the marketing mix

4.2.1. Scope of cultural influences on parts of the marketing mix

Companies that offer products to their customers have to plan several different components. The marketing mix, which includes the elements product, price, promotion as well as place, is an allocation of tasks a company has to plan when selling products.[154]

- Product: all decisions related to configuration of a product or service which is offered by a company
- Price: all aspects of agreements about prices, possible discounts and additional terms regarding delivery, payment and lending
- Promotion: all aspects of plan, design, coordination and control of all actions of a company related to its target groups to achieve marketing aims
- Place: all decisions related to planning, implementation and control of the distribution of products and services[155]

In the event that a company starts to sell a product abroad, marketers have to identify components of the marketing mix, and to which degree cultural differences in-

[154] Cf. Homburg, C., Krohmer, H. (2009), p. 7.
[155] Cf. Meffert, H., Burmann, C., Kirchgeorg, M. (2008), p. 397, 478, 562, 632.

fluence those components. As mentioned above, the degree of adaptation or standardisation varies for each industry. This aspect can also be transferred to the different parts of the marketing mix. Figure 6 shows a continuum of components of the marketing mix and the ease with which they can be standardised or adapted to local differences. It clearly shows that the strategy, image or product of a company can be standardised easily whereas pricing, distribution and promotion will more likely be adapted. Since culture is a subject of adaptation to local differences, one has to investigate to what degree culture has an effect on these three parts in connection to the theories by Hofstede and Hall.

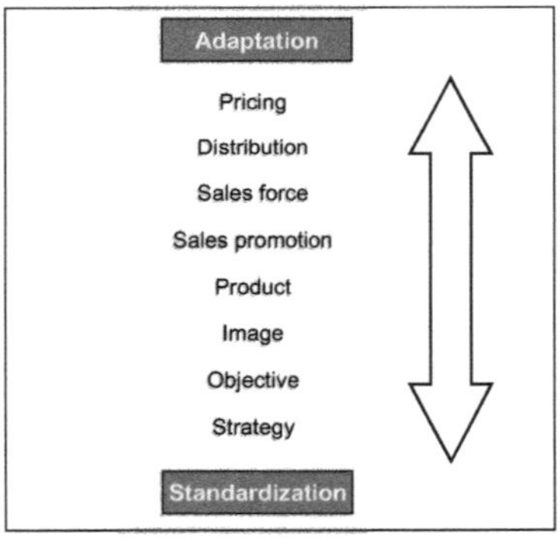

Figure 6: Continuum of standardisation vs. adaptation (source: Doole, I., Lowe, R., (2004), p. 200).

Since Hall developed his dimensions for cross-cultural communication and Hofstede's dimensions are primary used in a work-related environment where the relationship between people is also underlined by communication, it is appropriate to identify those of the three mentioned parts which are connected to communication at some point. According to the definitions provided at the beginning of this paragraph there are two parts which show a significant connection to communication issues.

Promotion of a company consists of various different components, namely advertising, public relations, sales force, sales promotion, event marketing, sponsoring and product placement.[156] All of these components share a common aspect: communication. As defined in section 3.2.1, Hall's theory provides a method for un-

[156] Cf. Gabler Wirtschaftslexikon (n.y.), http://wirtschaftslexikon.gabler.de/Archiv/10971/kommunikationspolitik-v11.html, accessed 13.05.2012.

derstanding cross-cultural communication, and so it seems to be an appropriate tool to understand cultural differences within promotion.

From this discussion it emerges that advertising seems to be especially vulnerable to cross-cultural issues. In 1996 Nancy Albers-Miller and Betsy Gelb argued that Hall's work, which has long been used for this matter, but also Hofstede's PDI, UAI, IDV and MAS dimensions, could be used to adapt advertising to cultural differences.[157] Mareike de Mooij, who also confirmed the relevance of Hofstede's dimensions for advertising across cultures, further supports this aspect.[158] Moreover, due to the high capital involvement, advertising is often said to be the most obvious as well as most important instrument of promotion. It is therefore important to investigate the influence of culture on advertising, as a failure can cause significant capital losses.[159]

ranking	country	absolut volume
1	USA	132,3
2	Japan	37,5
3	Germany	18,7
4	GB	18,7
5	France	9,2
6	Italy	7,4
7	Mexico	6,7
8	Canada	5,3
9	Brasil	5,2 (in Mrd. $)

Table 8: Expenditures on advertising of the 20 largest advertising markets (source: Müller, S., Gelbrich, K. (2004), p. 641).

Table 8 presents the results of a study published by ZAW in 2001 that shows that expenditures on advertising are especially high in the United States and Germany,

[157] Cf. Albers-Miller, N.D., Gelb, B.D. (1996).
[158] Cf. de Mooij, M., Hofstede, G. (2010), p. 102.
[159] Cf. Meffert, H., Burmann, C., Kirchgeorg, M. (2008), p. 649.

which rank in first and third place among the 20 largest advertising markets.[160] This further underlines the importance of investigating the influence of culture on advertising in both countries.

Place, or distribution, represents the second part of the marketing mix which is strongly affected by cultural differences. According to Usanier and Lee, distribution is even the part of the marketing mix which is most affected by cultural differences, since it is strongly connected to everyday life and the interaction and relationship between human beings.[161] Emrich supports this statement by pointing out that distribution is the one part which shows the least potential for standardisation because of cultural differences.[162]

Regarding distribution, companies have the choice between direct or indirect distribution of their product to the customer. In the process of direct distribution, companies often take over local firms to use them as distribution channels. In this case companies also acquire a local work force, which has a different cultural background and could cause problems between top-level management and employees. Moreover, the company is in direct contact with the customer through its own branches.

In contrast, in indirect distribution companies have frequent contact with local companies, for example sales agents or logistics companies. This also includes business negotiations with local persons from different cultures.[163] For both options, marketers need to be aware of cross-cultural communication issues. Again, Hofstede and Hall both provide tools to help identify and prepare a company's distribution strategy in terms of cross-cultural business negotiations. The potential of Hall's and Hofstede's theories for preparing business partners for cross-cultural negotiation has been sufficiently discussed and there is overall agreement that they provide appropriate tools for preparing cross-cultural business negotiations.[164]

---

[160] Cf. Müller, S., Gelbrich, K. (2004), p. 641.
[161] Cf. Usanier, J-C., Lee, J.A. (2009), p. 318.
[162] Cf. Emrich, Ch. (2009), p. 248.
[163] Cf. Meffert, H., Burmann, C., Kirchgeorg, M. (2008), p.562–574.
[164] Cf. LaBahn, W. D., Harich, K.R. (1994), Kale, S.H., Barnes, J.W. (1992).

According to table 6, the pricing of a good is easy to adapt to local differences. The hypothesis of effects of cultural differences on pricing strategies has also proven unpopular so far.[165]

Because culture consist of a large number of different parts, for instance values, assumptions and symbols, culture does have an effect on other parts of the marketing mix, for example on the product itself in terms of design or certain cultural symbols. However, this study exclusively focuses on the theories of Hall and Hofstede. Therefore, the analysis below examines how companies should develop their advertising as well as distribution strategy according to both theories.

4.2.2. Influence of culture on advertising

The following section describes the influence of cultural differences on advertising in the United States and Germany. It provides a theoretical framework for how companies should integrate cultural differences into their advertising strategy.

Advertising comprises communicational influence using the means of mass communication in various media with the aim to change the recipients' attitude towards the market in favour of the company's corporate objectives.[166] From the concepts of Hall and Hofstede several theoretical conclusions can be drawn about how marketers should conceive their advertising strategy in the United States and Germany. It is important to remember that both countries share a lot of similar characteristics, which are important to address. However, differences also exist and have to be carefully taken into consideration.

Advertising can be done in many ways, using different channels such as television, print media or social media. For the analysis of cross-cultural advertising in the United States and Germany this paper does not focus on one single channel, but rather provides general applications and examples for several different channels. From the above analysis of general cultural differences summarised in figure 4, one sees that advertising strategies for the two countries, according to Hall, can be similar in terms of context and time, whereas space and speed of message need to be differentiated.

[165] Cf. Burton, D. (2009), p. 185.
[166] Schweiger, G., Schrattenecker, G. (2005), p. 109.

Context

The first dimension that has an effect on advertising in the United States and Germany is context. Both countries are seen as rather low-context cultures, so it is important for marketers who try to market a product in one of those countries to focus on explicit communication. A study about the effect of cultures and advertising in the United States and Korea showed that there is a high tendency for low-context advertising in the United States. The study defined low-context advertising as having an emphasis on product features, utilitarian needs or the use of numbers.[167] Especially German advertising has to contain large amounts of facts about the product and features, because Germans are even more low-context than Americans.[168]

Whereas in high-context cultures marketers prefer symbols and indirect communication, they need to switch to a more rhetorical or argumentation-based style of advertising in the United States and Germany.[169] Because of their low-context culture, people in both countries need and at the same time accept a very direct form of addressing marketing statements or ideas, which shall be promoted with the help of an ad.

Time

Since both national cultures are monochromic, marketers should focus on only single or a few actions in advertising at the same time. Monochronic customers need to have the chance to process the messages an advertisement wants to transfer. If a customer is forced to process several different things at the same time there is the high possibility that he will not understand the message correctly or receive it at all. Due to the fact that the monochronic Americans and Germans like to divide tasks into smaller parts, one can derive that marketers should lead the customer through their commercial step by step to help them understand the core message. In conclusion, marketers should avoid overwhelming the American or the German customer in their advertising effort.

[167] Cf. Cho, B., et. al. (1999), p. 59–73.
[168] Cf. Hall, E., Hall, M. (1990), p.71.
[169] Cf. de Mooij, M. (2010), p. 71.

Space

A major difference between the United States and Germany is their concept of space. Due to their country's geographical size, Americans like spacious and big products. This can be seen in the American preference for large cars or houses. Therefore, in American advertising marketers should highlight the size of its products, for instance by comparing it to smaller competitors or mentioning the exact measurements. A study about American and German car ads by Bettina Temath, professor at the Technical University in Dortmund, showed that American car advertisements especially are more focused on space. She also argues that a lot of commercials in the United States include shots of wide landscapes and mountains, which reinforce the greater feeling of space and seize. Compared to the United States, German car ads focus more on the features rather than emotions. However, Temath also argues that American and German car advertising has also been affected by globalisation, resulting in a diluting of both characteristics over the last decades.[170]

Speed of message

Due to the different attitudes towards the speed of messages, marketers in the United States should pay more attention to fast messages like headlines, taglines or TV commercials. Marketers in the United States tend to use taglines in their advertising, addressing a fast message to promote their products. Germans on other hand are more focused on slow messages such as those in print advertising.[171]

In terms of Hofstede's dimensions the United States and Germany are similar in their attitude towards the PDI, IDV, MAS and LTO dimensions, whereas major differences occur in their attitude towards UAI. Especially the connection between values and advertising has often been used to show the effect of cultural differences on advertising by applying values to appeals.[172] Moriarty, Mitchell, and Wells say of appeal that it "connects with some emotion that makes the product

---

[170] Cf. Temath, B. (n.y.), http://www.tu-dortmund.de/uni/International/News/10-11-08_Car_Advertising/index.html, accessed 22.05.2012.
[171] Cf. Hall, E., Hall, M. (1990), p. 71.
[172] Cf. de Mooij, M. (2010), Albers-Miller, N.D., Gelb, B.D. (1996), Pollay, R. (1983).

particularly attractive or interesting, such as security, esteem, fear, sex, and sensory pleasure".[173] De Mooij argues that advertising is influenced by culture and can therefore be used to draw a connection between appeals and cultural values.[174] It is likely that if the consumer values and the advertising appeals share a significant subset, the advertising of products in connection to those values will be more effective than advertising which does not take this connection into account.[175] Accordingly, it seems appropriate to apply Hofstede's dimensions on advertising appeals to derive a connection between the theory and its effects on advertising.

PDI

Both countries in this study have a low power distance. According to de Mooij, low power distance countries do not have a strong need to market products as status symbols as is normal in high power distance countries like China. In contrast to high PDI environments, marketers should focus on appeals like freedom and independence. They should avoid appeals that evoke a feeling of inequality among people, for example by showing elder people giving advice to younger people.[176] Albers-Miller and Gelb, who based their work on a list of common cultural appeals provided by Pollay,[177] drew a connection between low PDI and appeals that promotes uniformity among people from those countries. According to them, it is better not to attract attention to someone's wealth but rather to try to reduce these differences in society. Low PDI countries also share a significant willingness to support others. Therefore, marketers should focus on appeals like humility and plainness.[178] Especially in the United States, marketers should also make use of the American Dream, which promotes the low power distance attitude of Americans and is therefore likely to be attractive to American customers in particular.

---

[173] Moriarty, S., Mitchel, N., Wells, W. (2009), p. 364.
[174] Cf. de Mooij, M. (2010), p. 217.
[175] Cf. Polegato, R, Bjerke, R. (2006), p. 263ff.
[176] Cf. de Mooij, M. (2010), p. 222.
[177] Cf. Pollay, R. (1983), p. 73ff.
[178] Cf. Albers-Miller, N.D., Gelb, B.D. (1996), p. 63.

IDV

Regarding the IDV dimension, marketers should focus on an individualistic advertising in both countries. A study on German and Chinese preferences in advertising found that the German customer is more attracted to individualistic values.[179] Similar results were found for the US in two other studies between Americans and North Koreans and between American and Chinese advertising. Cho argues that advertising should address appeals about the individuality or independence of the audience, focus on uniqueness, originality and hedonism, emphasise self-fulfilment, self-development or the benefits to the individual consumer.[180] Zhang and Neelankavil confirmed these findings in their study of the United States and China.[181]

As stated earlier, there is a correlation between the IDV dimension and context. This is most valid in terms of advertising. Advertising in the United States and Germany, which are both low-context individualistic countries, should be characterised by a very direct and personalised address, focusing on a frequent use of the personal pronouns I or my. Marketers in the United States and Germany should focus on appeals like personal benefits, success and achievements. Moreover, advertising should also promote individuality by focusing on single persons in ads, not on groups.

MAS

Masculine countries are characterised by their attitude towards success and ambition. Marketers in the United States and Germany should promote feelings like being the best and competition is good. Given the United States' score on the MAS dimension and the American attitude towards space, it can be derived that advertising with an emphasis on large and big products is more effective in the United States. Although the German score is similar on the MAS dimension, marketers should not apply the same aspect to the German market because of Germans' different feeling about space. Moreover, in both countries the typical images of male

[179] Cf. Diehl, S., Terlutter, R., Weinberg, P. (2003), pp. 128–136.
[180] Cf. Cho, B., et. al. (1999), pp. 59–73.
[181] Cf. Zhang, Y., Neelankavil, J.P. (1997), pp. 134–149.

and female should be promoted. There should be a strong differentiation between male- and female-related tasks like car washing or cooking.[182]

UAI

In the UAI dimension the United States and Germany differ. Therefore, marketers have to follow two different approaches in the two countries. In Germany, which is characterised by a relatively high degree of uncertainty avoidance, it should be more effective to stress appeals like durability and safety, for example in the safety features of cars.[183] There is also a need for high structure in ads as well as background information, which can for example prove the authenticity and applicability of products.

In comparison, the United States is a country that is more accepting of uncertainty. Americans are more open to innovations and new approaches or different ways of doing something. Marketers could for example use appeals like adventure and casualness. Due to this, as well as to the fact that low UAI countries prefer having few rules and regulations, potential customers will more likely be attracted to unconventional behaviour, which could be shown in American advertising.[184] Moreover, in contrast to German advertising, marketers in the United States should focus on the benefits of products rather than on the actual handling or the authenticity.

LTO

Judging by their scores on the LTO dimension both the American and the German are short-term oriented. This means that they do not have a high focus on saving for the future or long-term investments. However, the American customer is more short-term oriented. This should be addressed by offering instalment plans or discounts to customers in the advertisements to give more people the ability to buy products.[185] Due to their short-term orientation both countries show a strong con-

[182] Cf. de Mooij, M. (2010), p. 224ff.
[183] Cf. Albers-Miller, N.D., Gelb, B.D. (1996), p. 63.
[184] Cf. Albers-Miller, N.D., Gelb, B.D. (1996), p. 64.
[185] Cf. de Mooij, M. (2010), p. 234ff.

nection to traditions. Marketers should therefore include typical customs or traditions in their advertising concept to attract potential customers.

4.2.3. Examples of culture-related American and German advertising

The following section analyses advertising campaigns of American and German companies. The paper focuses on identifying culturally influenced print advertising, TV commercials and online advertising which reveal aspects of Hall's and Hofstede's models.

The United States and Germany share similar characteristics in terms of context, time, PDI, IDV, MAS as well as LTO. This does not mean that they are identical. There are differences even within these dimensions. However, for a general analysis such as this one the focus must lie on major differences and similarities. Because the cultures are similar it would be likely to find similarities in advertising campaigns from both countries. However, one should expect differences in space- and UAI-related aspects of advertising.

Nike Inc., an American sports apparel company, has used advertising that provides good examples of the concepts of low-context and individualism as well as their correlation. In 1988 Nike introduced a campaign which has become one of the success stories of Nike advertising. The campaign with the tagline *JUST DO IT* is a good example to show the cultural aspects discovered by Hall and Hofstede in advertising strategies. The tagline in figure 6 is a direct address to the customer, an explicit form of communication with the customer, as it is typical for low-context cultures like the United States and Germany.

Figure 7: Nike advertising "Just Do It" (source: Pope, S., (2011), www.adteachings.com, accessed 28.05.2012).

Nike used this tagline in several different ads that included famous persons like basketball or football stars. Figure 8 shows a print ad by Nike exemplifying the same effects of direct and explicit communication to the customer. It further has a very individualistic orientation by using the personal pronoun my. The tagline *MY ASSAULT* also emphasises the willingness to compete with others and being the best at what you do, promoting once again individualistic thinking. The individualistic character is also underscored by focusing on only one man in the advertising. The ad also stresses masculine appeals like advancement and challenge, which conform to both American as well as German culture.

Figure 8: Nike advertising "My Assault"
(source: http://www.adverbox.com/ads/nike-what-is-your-fight/, accessed 28.05.2012).

In another ad Nike uses the phrase *I AM THE BULLET IN THE CHAMBER* in connection to the tagline *JUST DO IT* to generate individualistic appeals like self-fulfilment and independence. The ad tries to imply that every athlete is responsible for his own success.

Figure 9: Nike advertising "I am the bullet in the chamber" (source: http://www.adverbox.com/ads/nike-what-is-your-fight/, accessed 28.05.2012).

Nike recently launched its new campaign, which once again has a focus on individualistic values with phrases like *MY TIME IS NOW # MAKE IT COUNT* (see figure 9). Nike again uses the personal pronoun my to appeal to the individual customer and his personal success and benefit.

Figure 10: Nike advertising "My time is now" (source: http://www.nike.com/nikeos/p/nike/en_US/?ref=, accessed 28.ß5.2012).

At first glance this ad seems to be collectivistic because of the presence of several people; however, a closer look reveals that those persons are all individual, famous football players, who are independent from one another. In connection with the tagline, the ad again displays an apparent individualistic concept.

German marketers use similar advertising strategies concerning the individualistic and low-context orientation. The ice-cream distributor Langnese and the Belgian ice-cream producer Magnum jointly published an ad with the tagline *I share a lot but not everything*. This also promotes individualistic values like hedonism as well as personal benefit.

Figure 11: Langnese advertising (source: De Mooij, (2010), p. 224).

Coke, an American beverage company, introduced a print ad for the German market that again promotes individualistic and low context characteristics. It addresses the customer in a direct and individualistic manner by using the personal pronoun Du (you).

Figure 12: Coke Light German advertising, (source: http://www.slogans.de/magazine.php?Op=Article&Id=155, accessed 13.06.2012).

Differences in the attitude towards space of Americans and Germans can be seen in advertising for cars. American car ads used to be more space–oriented, focusing on the features connected to e.g. spacious storage rooms or the measurements of the car in general. Acura, a subsidiary of Japanese car manufacturer Honda Motor Company, provides a good example for this aspect.

Figure 13: Acura advertising (source: http://www.judycasey.com/news/category/SUV, accessed 30.05.2012).

Acura published an advertisement for the American market that emphasises the size of the car. As one can see from figure 10 the ad promotes the feeling that an entire life can fit into the newly developed car.

In addition, in an ad for the American market the German car manufacturer Audi also stresses the measurements of their largest SUV, the Q7 (see figure 11). This aspect is further underlined by the similar tagline *Big can be beautiful.* in the main frame of the ad as well as in the information text below the ad. However, this ad also shows aspects of the German cultural preference for technical facts. The tagline F*rom the creator of the Quattro.* emphasises the technical features of the car. There is also a hint of a traditional orientation in this tagline, which reflects American as well as German short-term orientation. Audi uses this slogan in various ads for its cars, thereby connecting them all to technical features as well as their special Audi tradition.

Figure 14: Audi advertising Q7 (source: http://www.productioncars.com/dx5/vintage_car_ads3.php?make2=Audi&model2=Q7, accessed 30.05.2012).

There are some differences in car advertising in Germany; however, differences in the space orientation are not obvious. For example, Volkswagen published an advertising campaign *Danke Mann* for their Touareg that focused on space by showing wide landscapes and mountains. According to the research conducted by Bettina Temath, these values were formerly used in American car ads. This is a good example supporting her findings that American and German car advertising has grown increasingly similar in the promoted values.

A print ad of Hummer, an American car company, emphasises Americans' uncertainty-accepting attitude. In figure 13 marketers tried to create an adventure image surrounding the car. The ad implies that the customer can drive everywhere with this car. The destination is not fixed, there is no certainty about where to go, underlining the adventurous character of this ad. Due to Americans' uncertainty acceptance this type of ad should be more attractive to them than to the German customer.

Germans are from an uncertainty-avoiding culture, meaning that they try to create certainty as much as possible. Beauty or health care products especially highlight this aspect. Companies selling those products often commission independent laboratories, like Stiftung Warentest, to verify the positive effects of their products. The results are often mentioned in the ads, as seen in figure 14. This creates certainty for the German customer, convincing him to buy this product.

Figure 15: Hummer advertising (source: http://www.productioncars.com/vintage-ads.php/Hummer/H2, accessed 01.06.2012).

Figure 16: Pantene advertising (source: http://www.youtube.com/watch?v=LfCwfpkytys, accessed 01.06.2012).

This aspect also underlines the general concept of advertising in both countries. Whereas German advertising tries to give information and facts about the product, American advertising tends to be more emotional by hyping the product.[186]

Both countries share a monochronic time orientation, which is reflected in the online advertising efforts in both countries. McDonalds in both countries uses a monochronic structure on the websites advertising their products. The customer is led through the entire website and its advertising strategies for products, which are only shown step by step. The customer can switch between products or special promotions. Although sometimes more than one product is shown at the same time, the website always tries to focus on only one main aspect, such as the special offer for a McDeal menu (see figure 17). The website is well-structured, and different navigation tools help the customer to continue to the next step. This helps American and German customers focus on one single message at a time, and ensures that they receive the intended message. The same characteristics can be found in advertising on the American website of Audi. Again, most of the attention is given to one single aspect in the centre of the website, and the customer can use navigation tools to move step by step (see figure 18).

Figure 17: McDonalds advertising (source: www.mcdonalds.de, accessed 01.06.2012).

[186] Cf. Hall, E., Hall, M. (1990), p. 169.

Figure 18: Audi homepage advertising (source: http://progress.audiusa.com/, accessed 14.06.2012).

4.2.4. Influence of culture on distribution

The following section describes cultural patterns, which affect the distribution of products in the United States and Germany by pointing out the similarities and the differences between both countries. It provides a theoretical framework for companies to integrate these cultural differences into their business negotiations with distributors, working with employees from different cultures as well as their direct contact to the customer.

Distribution is, by definition, the overall economic allocation of goods, services, rights, charges and information. It includes all processes between a producer and sales agents, up to the customer through the sales channel.[187] One of the most important advantages of direct distribution is the immediate communication with the customer.[188] However, this advantage can become a major problem in cross-cultural distribution. As in direct distribution, the indirect approach also can lead

[187] Cf. Gabler Wirtschaftslexikon (n.y.), http://wirtschaftslexikon.gabler.de/Archiv/56409/distribution-v5.html, accessed 30.05.2012.

[188] TEIA (n.y.), http://www.teialehrbuch.de/Kostenlose-Kurse/Marketing/15336-Direkter-und-indirekter-Vertrieb.html, accessed 08.06.2012.

to communication issues because more than one party is involved. In this process, a company's choice of direct or indirect distribution will determine whether most of its communications are with customers or with sales agents. However, both consist of interactions between the company and outsiders. Problems can arise when the company and the customer are not from the same cultural background. The same applies for local staff when a company enters a market by taking over local companies to distribute its products.

A Canadian study found that about 63 per cent of companies engaged in export sales distribute their products in a foreign market through the same channels as in their domestic market.[189] However, it is important for companies to evaluate to which degree culture has an effect on distribution, as this could significantly affect the choice and the handling of distribution channels.

The cultural effects on distribution have been widely discussed. A study by Douglas W. LaBahn and Katrin R. Harich investigating the relationship between American companies and Mexican distributors showed that cultural sensitivity and communication are significant elements of cross-cultural distribution. According to the study, cultural sensibility is a major factor for successful cross-cultural distribution.[190] Kale and Barnes conducted another study about the cultural impact on distribution that identified the high importance of culture.[191] Since Hall and Hofstede both provide a model which helps to become aware of cultural differences, it seems reasonable to help marketers gain this cultural sensibility. As mentioned earlier, the United States and Germany share similar characteristics in terms of context, time, PDI, IDV, MAS as well as LTO. But it is important to remember that this does not mean that they are identical. There are also differences in those dimensions. However, for a general analysis the focus lies on major differences and similarities.

Context:

As stated earlier, both countries share low-context characteristics. In both direct and indirect distribution, communication with foreign sales agents and customers

[189] Cf. McNaughton R, Bell J. (2001), p. 24–39.
[190] Cf. LaBahn, W. D., Harich, K.R. (1994).
[191] Cf. Kale, S.H., Barnes, J.W. (1992), p. 101–132.

should be conducted in a low-context manner. This generally means a formal, explicit, bottom up, deductive reasoning, leading to a conclusion during business negotiations by using facts, objective arguments and an emphasis on skills to convince the interlocutor.[192] Both countries require very explicit and direct language in negotiations, but also in the terms of contracts. In both countries it is appropriate to avoid symbolic communication and a focus on facial expressions or general body language.

American and German businesses expect to receive a clear and determined answer to inquiries and questions.[193] However, Germans may provide more background information than Americans, which may create feelings that they believe others to be under-educated. As mentioned above, Germans like to use examples in their communication, so it is important to support presentations and discussions with proper examples. For American companies it may also be advantageous to learn German, since Germans believe that if you are not able to speak a language at all you should not do business in that country.[194] In contrast, Germans should be aware that Americans try to exaggerate a lot in their way of communicating.[195]

Time

Due to their monochronic time concept, both cultures need to conceive their business negotiations as well as their interaction with other employees in a structured way to be most effective. Germans in particular are very time-oriented and believe in a precise scheduling of business meetings and negotiations. Although Americans are generally monochromic, it is important for German companies to remember that the United States consists of a broad variety of different cultures and that there is a high possibility that they meet people from a different cultural background such as Latin America, who are said to be polychronic.[196]

Another difference is that Americans try to seal a deal in a very short time because time is valued in money. Therefore, they try to reduce unnecessary formalities to

[192] Cf. Manrai, L.A. Manrai, A.K. (2010), p. 90.
[193] Cf. Salacuse, J.W. (2004), p. 3.
[194] Cf. Hall, E. T., Hall, M.R. (1990), 49f.
[195] Cf. Hall, E. T., Hall, M.R. (1990), p. 146.
[196] Ibid, p. 35, p. 140.

focus on the actual business.[197] In comparison, German businesses need significantly more time to make a decision and agree to a business deal; this is caused by their preference for an elaborate background research. Therefore, it is also important to remember that once a plan has been made German managers will not change it.[198]

Space

As in advertising, the different attitudes towards space are also valid in terms of business negotiations in indirect distribution and in contacts with the customer in direct distribution. For Germans, personal space and privacy is more important than for Americans. The fact that Germans like to address each other with their last names underlines this aspect. Also, Germans are not used to smile to strangers a lot, and the physical distance between two persons to feel comfortable is larger than in the United States. In direct contacts with the customer, American companies in Germany should keep a certain distance to try to avoid invading their customers' personal space. This also applies for tasks which are exclusively for the customer.

Although Americans also keep their personal distance, they need a smaller personal space than Germans. Since smiling to strangers is more common, it is also allowed to greet and smile a lot to customers in shops. It is also permitted to address the customer directly, using an impersonal approach.[199] The same aspects hold true in business negotiation. The personal space of managers in Germany is more important than in American businesses, so a direct impersonal address in Germany is not appropriate, whereas American managers prefer this approach. German managers like to address their business partners by their titles and try to avoid talks about personal topics like family or private life in general. In contrast, Americans like to build a personal and friendly atmosphere during the negotiation process.[200]

---

[197] Cf. Salacuse, J.W. (2004) p. 3.
[198] Cf. Hall, E.T., Hall, M.R. (1990), p. 35.
[199] Cf. Hall, E.T., Hall, M.R. (1990), p. 39f, 141f.
[200] Cf. Salacuse, J.W. (2004) p. 2.

Speed of messages

Since Americans are accustomed to fast messages it can take a while for Germans to get the point of a discussion in a negotiation. Americans are also used to the headline style; they announce at the start of a presentation what they are going to talk about. Americans should repeat the main points of a speech at the end of a presentation to make sure that the Germans business partner doesn't miss a point. This is not only important in presentation but also at the end of business negotiations.[201] In this case the dimensions speed of message and time are correlated to the pace at which Germans and Americans try to seal deals. Germans have a slower pace than Americans, who should keep this in mind when negotiating with German companies.

A study conducted by Kale and McIntyre drew connections between distribution and Hofstede's 4 dimensions PDI, IDV, MAS and UAI, applying them to three stages of channel distribution: initiation process, implementation process and review process. They also provide propositions for companies engaging in cross-cultural channel relationship.[202] Moreover, Foster connected cross-cultural business negotiation styles with Hofstede's dimensions model.[203] Additionally, Hofstede conducted his work primarily for the work environment. Therefore, it seems to offer a good framework for identifying differences and similarities in terms of business negotiations between a company and its distributors or the relationship between employees from different cultural backgrounds.

PDI

The process of gaining access to a network in the initial process of business negotiations differs in low and high PDI countries. Both the United States and Germany are low PDI countries. Müller and Gelbrich introduced the thesis that low PDI and high IDV countries try to find a partner within similar countries, so that it is

[201] Cf. Hall, E.T., Hall, M.R. (1990), p. 49.
[202] Cf. Kale, S.H., McIntyre, R.P. (1993), p. 31–45.
[203] Cf. Foster, D.A. (1995).

easy in both countries to get into contact with potential business partners.[204] In the United States as well as in Germany, both sides focus on an equal contract and a joint decision-making process. Due to their low PDI, business negotiations in both countries suffer less interference from top-level managers; they are a lively discussion to which every member equally contributes. Moreover, PDI cultures are said to engage in a more communication-based discussion and focus on vis-à-vis communication.[205] Companies from both countries appreciate competence and expect a consulting management style.[206] The same aspects apply for the relationship between managers and employees from a different cultural background.

IDV

Both countries are individualistic, so their business negotiation style should be similar in this point. Kale and McIntyre argue that in business negotiations individualistic cultures try to focus on personal interest and on performance. American and German companies will be more self-centred and opposed to their distribution partners. They expect their counterparts to look after themselves and promote their own self-interest. The conflicts that arise due to that behaviour are typical and are accepted. Moreover, American and German companies will both reward a positive partnership with a distributor, whereas they will try to blame the partner for a negative outcome.[207] Graham and Lam assembled a list of characteristics using the example of the United States to show how individualistic countries approach contract negotiation. They argue that individualistic countries aim is to make a good deal, and pursue this aim with aggressive and impatient argumentation.[208] Those findings are also applicable to management and employee relationships.

MAS

Both countries are masculine countries, so earnings, recognition, advancement and challenge characterise their business negotiations and business relationships. Peo-

---

[204] Cf. Müller, S., Gelbrich, K. (2004), p. 775.
[205] Cf. Kale, S.H., McIntyre, R.P. (1993), p. 38.
[206] Cf. Foster, D.A. (1995), p. 265f.
[207] Cf. Kale, S.H., McIntyre, R.P. (1993), p. 36ff.
[208] Cf. Graham, J.L., Lam, N.M. (2003), p. 4.

ple from these countries are generally more attracted to an assertive and aggressive atmosphere.[209] In business negotiations, companies from both countries can expect this climate for negotiations. In addition, they focus much more on financial rewards, and relationships between the company and distributors are more easily cancelled. Due to the fact that masculine cultures tend to be more aggressive and competition-oriented, companies do not want to build on a co-operational base but try to gain the largest benefits for themselves. When valuing a relationship between the company and a distributor, companies from both countries focus more on the actual financial outcome and not on the relationship itself.[210]

UAI

Uncertainty avoidance is a major difference between the two countries and is therefore also important in terms of business negotiations and employee relationships. As stated earlier, Germans need significantly more time and background information to make a decision. Their generally uncertainty-avoiding character further underlines this aspect. German managers and employees want to be sure to minimise the risks, whereas Americans often require little background information, leading them to make faster decisions.[211] This could have a major impact on the success or failure of business negotiations as well as on relationships with employees.

Kale and McIntyre address this aspect by proposing that uncertainty-accepting managers from American companies show a high degree of flexibility during negotiations, whereas German companies investigate the background of a potential partner more carefully, resulting in a conscious decision. In terms of the outcome of a partnership between the company and a distributor, German companies would measure the overall performance of that partnership.[212]

---

[209] Cf. Hofstede, G. (1991), p. 81f.
[210] Cf. Kale, S.H., McIntyre, R.P. (1993), p. 37ff.
[211] Cf. Foster, D.A. (1995), p. 268f.
[212] Cf. Kale, S.H., McIntyre, R.P. (1993), p. 37ff.

LTO

Both countries share a short-term attitude according to their score in this dimension. Companies from both cultures want to achieve quick results and are interested in rather short – term relationships between their company and a distributor. This contrasts with Hall's time dimension, where Germany needs much more time to gather background information and make a decision.

4.2.5. Wal-Mart as a negative example of cross-cultural distribution

Although the results of the cultural analysis of the United States and Germany show significant similarities in their attitude towards the dimensions of Hall and Hofstede, there remain differences which, at first glance, seem to be minor compared to the similarities. However, companies that try to enter one of these markets often seem to struggle. An example is the American retail company Wal-Mart Inc.. Wal-Mart has been a success in the United States for several decades, mainly because of their unique distribution system. However, their approach to the German market ended in a pull-out in 2006.[213]

Emrich identified two different groups of issues that caused this unsuccessfully market entry. On the one hand, there were problems in their overall internationalisation strategy of takeovers, underestimation of the German competition as well as possibilities to expand. On the other hand, some problems had a cultural background, like their ignorance of German legislation power, failed human resource management and the existence of language barriers, a standardised American corporate culture and ignorance of cultural values of German employees and customers.[214] According to the findings of the analysis presented here, failures were to be expected due to Hall's dimensions of space and speed of message as well as Hofstede's UAI dimension.

Wal-Mart offered the German customers the service that an employee packed their groceries into a bag at the cashier's and carried them to their cars. Because of Germans attitude towards privacy and personal space, customers perceived this

[213] Cf. Christopherson, S. (2007), p. 451.
[214] Cf. Emrich, C. (2009), p. 251ff.

special service as an invasion of their personal space and privacy. The same problem arose with the so-called *Greeters*. These were employees who were responsible for greeting customers with a smile at the entrance to inform them about special offers. As stated earlier, Germans also feel uncomfortable when strangers smile a lot at them.

Another aspect was Wal-Mart's so-called ten-foot rule. This rule stated that if a customer came within ten feet of an employee, this employee had to offer his help to the customer. In a survey about the failures of Wal-Mart, German customers answered that they felt surprised and under observation because of this service.[215] Another individual Wal-Mart ritual was the so-called *Morning Cheer*. In this ritual, all employees and the store manager had to come together and shout the Wal-Mart chant like a cheerleading group. German employees were not accustomed to showing emotions at work, since cheering and dancing is exclusively done in private life.

It was also unacceptable to German managers to share their bedrooms on business travels, as was the rule at the beginning of Wal-Mart's operations in Germany.[216] In all of these aspects, it was differences in the attitudes towards space which caused the problems. German customers and employees felt an invasion of personal space and privacy.

Wal-Mart took over several branches of the German retailers Wertkauf and Interspar including some of their local staff. However, they did not appoint a German manager as CEO; the first four were Americans. Rob Tiarks, the first CEO, did not speak any German, showed no effort to learn it and had no experience in the German retail market.[217] He introduced English as the official language at Wal-Mart Germany, which caused a rapidly increasing fluctuation among German managers.[218] Wal-Mart tried to impose its cultural values on German employees, instead of adapting to local cultural differences by appointing a German speaker, or at least an expert in the German market. As discussed in the previous section, Germans believe that a foreign businessman should at least speak German to be successful. Moreover, Wal-Mart made decisions at a very high pace to positively influence their net earnings; for instance, they reduced salaries in 2006. However,

---

[215] Cf. Gerhard, U. Hahn, B. (2005), p. 23.
[216] Cf. Senge, K. (2004), p. 13.
[217] Cf. Knorr, A., Arndt, A. (2003), p. 9ff.
[218] Cf. Emrich, C. (2009), p. 252.

Germans need to obtain more background information and consultations with stakeholder and therefore take more time to decide on issues.[219]

As stated above, Germans try to avoid uncertainty as much as possible, whereas Americans accept uncertainty to a certain degree. This can be seen in Wal-Mart's slogan, *Let's do it*. It implies that they do not need a very well-structured plan, but rather carry out things without thinking and planning too much, even if this means taking some risks.[220] Along with other mistakes, for example the defiance of several laws, all of the mentioned cultural factors played an important role in Wal-Mart's performance in Germany.

5. Conclusion

5.1. Achievement of goals

The large amount of literature concerning cultural differences and marketing shows the importance of this topic. It has been discussed for several decades. However, there are companies that do not appreciate these differences; but they ignore the studies at their own risk.

The fact that there are several different definitions of culture is also apparent from the studied literature. Often scientists and researchers apply general, superficial cultural differences like colour preferences or the language itself. Hall's and Hofstede's models, however, provide a much deeper, more profound theory. Although they were not initially developed for marketing, they can be used to investigate how cultural differences affect the marketing mix in some points.

It is difficult to find the right derivations for some areas of marketing. In this process, advertising and distribution showed the most potential for cultural influence. Moreover, the two different models have contrary findings in some points. For example, according to Hall's time and speed of message dimensions Germans need significantly more time to decide on topics. In contrast, Hofstede states that Germany is short-term oriented, with a focus on quick results. Nonetheless, these theories embody a tool to reduce the effects of the SRC, which is an important barrier

[219] Cf. Christopherson, S. (2007), p. 458.
[220] Cf. Berggoetz, R., Laue, M. (2002), p. 7.

to successful marketing abroad. Therefore, American as well as German companies can use them to become aware of the differences between their own culture and others.

The two countries share significant similarities in terms of context, time as well as PDI, IDV, MAS and LTO. The large degree of similarities, however, does not mean that they are identical. Differences also occur in those dimensions. Still, these findings show that standardisation between the United States and Germany could be an option.

Regarding advertising, the studied examples show connections between theory and practice, between Hall's and Hofstede's dimensions and both countries' advertising. Most ads are similar, especially in terms of IDV, context and time, which is coherent with other studies. The cultural differences concerning space and UAI are also visible in the advertising. This implies that companies like Audi adapted their advertising to the American attitude towards space. However, the dilution effect of globalisation revealed by the research conducted by Temath is also valid, and can be seen in the example of the Volkswagens Touareg campaign.

Cultural differences and their effects on distribution are often underestimated, because at first glance they do not show a significant impact on revenues or the performance of a company. However, on second glance it becomes obvious that those differences have a major impact on the overall performance, especially in the case of takeovers of local companies, direct contact to the customer or business negotiations with local sales agents and distributors.

Due to the fact that both countries share a significant part of their cultures, distribution as well as business negotiations show a certain potential for standardisation. However, to successfully distribute their product in the United States and Germany, companies have to adapt to differences in their attitude towards space and UAI. In the case of Wal-Mart, the ignorance of those two dimensions in particular let to an overall failure of their market entry in Germany. Wal-Mart did not adapt its distribution strategy to the German culture at all. The SRC is one issue that American managers were not familiar with. They projected their American values onto the German managers as well as the customers. The analysis of Wal-Mart's market entry into Germany reveals issues with cultural differences, especially in terms of space and UAI. Those issues were one major factor for Wal-Mart's withdrawal from the German market.

Even though both cultures show a large number of similarities, it is important to identify all cultural differences that have an effect on marketing, especially in advertising and distribution. In light of the discussion about standardisation or adaptation, the proposition is that, rather than choosing between the two, companies should use both simultaneously. This also underlines the difficult distinction between international marketing and global marketing. Even global players like the Coca Cola Company adapt parts of their marketing mix to local cultural differences. The aim of global marketing should not be no adaptation at all but a more compromise-ready attitude based on adaptation where they are appropriate and necessary. Therefore, international marketing and global marketing become indistinguishable in terms of standardisation and adaptation to cultural differences.
This is also valid for the United States and Germany. The crucial element is to identify the areas of similarity and the areas of divergence. The next step is then to decide to what degree the company should standardise or adapt to the foreign culture. This approach generates the most possible scale effects while decreasing the risk of failure due to cultural differences. This approach should be most beneficial for American as well as German companies trying to sell products in each other's countries.

5.2. Outlook and perspectives

The process of globalisation will not stop in the near future; in fact it is likely that the speed at which this process evolves will further increase. One of the main points of criticism of both cultural theories is their lack of current data. The study by Temath shows that a dilution of values in car advertising has already begun. It should be investigated to which degree this is also valid in other industries. The culture and management consultancy Itim International conducts a survey on its website asking if the world is about to become a global culture, which could be one of the result of this dilution effect.[221]
This question is a good starting point for further studies on this topic. It is important to investigate whether the world is on the road to become a global culture, to what degree this global culture may already exists and, if it does, how fast it

[221] Cf. Itim International (n.y.), http://geert-hofstede.com/, accessed 18.07.2012

will still grow. A similar research to Hofstede's 5 dimensions model but with more up to data would help to investigate this issue. With regards to the present analysis of different examples of advertising, it is important to further investigate empirically how coherent the findings are throughout several different product types and industries. Moreover, the findings should be tested against other cultural theories, for example Trompenaars' 7 dimensions model.

Bibliography

Albers-Miller, N.D., Gelb, B.D. (1996): Business Advertising Appeals as a Mirror of Cultural Dimensions: A Study of Eleven Countries, in: Journal of Advertising, Vol. 25, Issue 4, pp. 57–70

Appadurai, A. (2003): Modernity at Large: Cultural Dimensions in Globalization, Minneapolis, 2003

Balbaaki, I.B., Malhorta, N.K. (1995): Standardization versus Customization in International Marketing: An Investigation Using Bridging Conjoint Analysis, in: Journal of the Academy of Marketing Science, Vol. 23, issue 3, pp. 182–194

Berggoetz, R., Laue, M. (2002): Wal-Mart's Market Entry into Germany from an Intercultural Perspective, in: European Retail Digest, Volume 34, p. 6

Bond, M.H. (1988): Finding universal dimensions of individual variation in multicultural studies of values: The Rokeach and Chinese value surveys, in: Journal of Personality and Social Psychology, Vol. 55, Issue 6, pp. 1009–1015

Bradley, F. (2002): International Marketing Strategy, 4th edition, Essex, 2002

Brei, V.A., D'Avila, L., Camargo, L.F., Engels, J. (2011): The influence of Adaptation and Standardization of the Marketing Mix on Performance: a Meta-Analysis, in: Brazilian Administration Review, Vol. 8, No.3, Art. 3, pp. 266–287

Burton, D. (2009): Cross-Cultural Marketing: theory, practice and relevance, New York, Abingdon, 2009

Cateora, P.R., Graham, J.L. (2002): International Marketing, 11th edition, New York, 2002

Christopherson, S. (2007): Barriers to 'US style' lean retailing: the case of Wal-Mart's failure in Germany, in: Journal of Economic Geography, Volume 7, Issue 4, pp. 451–469

Cho, B, Kwon, U, Gentry, J, Jun, S, & Kropp, F. (1999): Cultural Values Reflected in Theme and Execution: A Comparative Study of U.S. and Korean Television Commercials, in: Journal of Advertising, Vol. 28, No. 4, pp. 59–73

Czinkota, M.R., Ronkainen, I.A. (2007): International Marketing, 8th edition, Mason, 2007

Diehl, S., Terlutter, R., Weinberg, P. (2003): Advertising effectiveness in different cultures: Results of an experiment analysing the effects of individualistic and collectivistic advertising on Germans and Chinese, in: European Advances in Consumer Research, Vol. 6, pp.128–136

Doole, I., Lowe, R. (2008): International Marketing Strategy: Analysis, Development and Implementation, 5th edition, 2008

Emrich, Ch. (2009): Interkulturelles Marketing-Management, 2nd edition, Wiesbaden, 2009

Ferraro, G., Andreatta, S. (2010): Cultural Anthropology: An Applied Perspective, 8th edition, Belmont, 2010

Ford, D., Moore III, J, Milner, R. (2005): Beyond Cultureblindness: A Model of Culture With Implications for Gifted Education, in: Roeper Review, Vol. 27, No. 2, pp. 97–103

Foster, D.A. (1995): Bargaining Across Borders: How to Negotiate Business Successfully Anywhere in the World, (n.l.), 1995

Gerhard, U., Hahn, B. (2005): Wal-Mart and Aldi: Two retail giants in Germany, in: GeoJournal, Vol. 62, pp. 15–26

Ghemawat, P. (2007): Managing Differences, The Central Challenge of Global Strategy, in: Harvard Busines Review, (n.v.)

Graham, J.L., Lam, N.M. (2003): The Chinese Negotiation, in: Harvard Business Review, (n.v.)

Hall, E. T. (1976): Beyond Culture, New York, 1976

Hall, E.T. (1981): The silent language, New York, Toronto, 1981

Hall, E.T., Hall, M.R. (1990): Understanding Cultural Differences, keys to success in West Germany, France and the United States; 16th edition, Boston, London,

Hofstede, G. (1980): Culture's Consequences, International Differences in Work – Related Values, Beverly Hills, 1990

Hofstede, G. (2003): Cultures and Organizations: Software of the Mind: Intercultural Cooperation and Its Importance for Survival, London, 2003

Homburg, C., Krohmer, H. (2009): Marketingmanagement, Strategie – Instrumente – Umsetzung – Unternehmensführung, 3rd edition, Wiesbaden, 2009

Jain, S. C. (2007): State of the art of international marketing research: directions for the future, in: Journal of Global Business Advancement, Vol. 1, Issue 1, pp. 4–19

Jandt, F. E. (2010): An introduction to intercultural communication: Identities in global community, 6th edition, Thousand Oaks, London, New Delhi et. al., 2010

Kale, S.H., Barnes, J.W. (1992): Understanding The Domain of Cross-National Buyer-Seller Interactions, in: Journal of International Business Studies 1992, Vol. 23, No. 1, pp. 101–132

Knorr, A., Arndt, A., (2003): Why did Wal-Mart fail in Germany?, in: Materialien des Wissenschaftsschwerpunktes "Globalisierung der Weltwirtschaft", Vol. 24

Kotabe, M., Helsen, K. (2009): The SAGE Handbook of International Marketing, London, Thousand Oaks, New Delhi et al., 2009

Kotabe, M., Helsen, K. (2011): Global Marketing Management, 5th edition, Hoboken, 2011

Kroeber, A.L, Kluckhohn, C. (1952): Culture – A Critical Review of Concepts and Definitions, New York, 1952

Lee, J.A. (1966): Cultural Analysis in Overseas Operations, in: Harvard Business Review, (n.v.)

Levitt, T. (1983): "The Globalization of Markets" in: Harvard Business Review, (n.v.)

Manrai, L.A., Manrai A.K. (2010): The influence of Culture in International Business Negotiations: A New conceptual Framework and Managerial Implications, in: Journal of Transnational Management, Vol. 15, pp. 69–100

Marshall Matthews, B. (2000): The Chinese Value Survey: An interpretation of value scales and consideration of some preliminary results, in: International Education Journal, Vol. 1. No. 2, pp. 117–126

McNaughton, R., Bell, J. (2001): Channel Switching between Domestic and Foreign Markets, in: Journal of International Marketing, Vol. 9, Issue 1, pp. 24–39

McSweeney, B. (2002): Hofstede's model of national cultural differences and their consequences: A triumph of faith - a failure of analysis, in: Human Relations, Vol. 55, Issue 1, pp. 89–118,

Meffert, H., Burmann, C., Kirchgeorg, M. (2008): Marketing, Grundlagen marktorientierter Unternehmensführung, Konzepte – Instrumente – Praxisbeispiele, 10th edition, Wiesbaden, 2008

de Mooij, M. (2010): Global Marketing and Advertising, Understanding Cultural Paradoxes, 3rd edition, Thousand Oaks, 2010

de Mooij, M., Hofstede, G. (2010): The Hofstede Model, Application to global branding and advertising strategy and research, in: International Journal of Advertising 2010, Vol. 29, Issue 1, pp.85–110

Moriarty, S., Mitchell, N., Wells, W. (2009): Advertising: Principles and practice, 8th edition, Upper Saddle River, 2009

Müller, S., Gelbrich, K. (2004): Interkulturelles Marketing, München, 2004

O'Connel, J. (1997): The Blackwell Encyclopaedic Dictionary of International Management, Malden, 1997

Polegato, R., Bjerke,R. (2006): The link between cross-cultural value associations and liking: The case of Benetton and its advertising, in: Journal of Advertising, Vol. 46, Issue 3, pp. 236–273

Pollay, R. W. (1983): Measuring the Cultural Values Manifest in Advertising, in: Current Issues and Research in Advertising, Vol. 6.1, pp.71–92

Salacuse, J.W. (2004): Negotiating: The top ten ways that culture can affect your negotiation, in: Ivey Business Journal, (n.v.)

Samovar, L., Porter, R., McDaniel, E. (2012): Intercultural Communication: A Reader, 13th edition, Boston, 2012

Sands, R., Bourjolly, J, Roer-Strier, D. (2007): Cross Cultural Barriers in Research Interviewing, in: Qualitative Social Work, Vol. 6, Issue 3

Schmidt, P. (2010): Geert Hofstede, An interview with a pioneer in cross-cultural studies, in: Sietar Europe Newsletter September 2010

Schweiger, G., Schrattenecker, G. (2005): Werbung. Eine Einführung, 6th edition, Stuttgart, 2005

Sela-Sheffy, R., Shlesinger, M. (2011): Identity and status in the translational profession, Amsterdam, Philadelphia, 2011

Senge, K. (2004): Der Fall Wal-Mart: Institutionelle Grenzen ökonomischer Globalisierung, working paper no. 4, Juli 2004, Universität Dortmund (publisher)

Shah, S. J.A. (2004): The Researcher/Interviewer in Intercultural Context: a social intruder, in: British Educational Research Journal, Vol. 30, Issue 4, pp. 549–575

Shankarmahesh, M. (2006): Consumer ethnocentrism: an integrative review of its antecedents and consequences, in: International Marketing Review, Vol. 23, Issue 2, pp. 146–172

Shimp, A., Sharma, S. (1987): Consumer Ethnocentrism: Construction and Validation of the CETSCALE, in: Journal of Marketing Research, Vol. XXIV, pp. 280–290

Soares, A.M., Farhangmehr, M., Shoham, A. (2007): Hofstede's dimensions of culture in international marketing studies, in: Journal of Business Research, Volume. 60, pp. 277–284

Sumner, G.A. (1906): Folkways, A Study of the Sociological Importance of Usages, Manners, Customs, Mores, and Morals, New York, 1906

Trompenaars, F., Hampden –Turner, C. (1995): Riding the Waves of Culture, 2nd edition, London, Naperville, 1995

Usanier, J-C., Lee, J.A. (2009): Marketing Across Cultures, 5th edition, Essex, 2009

Wederspahn, G. (2000): Intercultural Services – A Worldwide Buyer´s Guide and Sourcebook, Houston, 2000

Xie, A., Rau, P., Tseng, Y., Su, H., Zhao, C. (2008): Cross-cultural influence on communication effectiveness and user interface design, in: International Journal of Intercultural Relations, Volume 33, Issue 1, pp. 11–20

Zhang, Y., Neelankavil, J.P. (1997): The influence of culture on advertising effectiveness in China and the USA: A cross-cultural study, in: European Journal of Marketing, Volume 31, Issue 2, pp. 134–149

Electronic Bibliography

Adler, N. (2004): Communicating across Cultural Barriers, accessible at http://www.radford.edu/~kvharring/docs/HRMDocs/5comm.pdf, accessed 17.04.2012

Centre for Intercultural Learning (n.y.): http://www.international.gc.ca/cfsi-icse/cil-cai/magazine/v02n01/doc3-eng.pdf, accessed 06.07.2012

Clearly Cultural (n.y.): Making Sense of Cross Cultural Communication, Geert Hofstede cultural dimensions, http://www.clearlycultural.com/geert-hofstede-cultural-dimensions/, accessed 20.04.2012

Cultural GPS Lite (n.y.): A global positioning system to navigate through intercultural differences based on the 5-D model of Professor Hofstede, Apple iPad application, accessed May 2012

Frericks, R. (n.y.): Cultural patterns, downloaded from Landesakademie für Fortbildung und Personalentwicklung an Schulen, http://lehrerfortbildung-bw.de/bs/bsa/bgym/kompcult/culpat/cultural-patterns.ppt, accessed 17.04.2012

Gabler Wirtschaftslexikon (n.y.): keyword: Economies of Scale, http://wirtschaftslexikon.gabler.de/Archiv/54610/economies-of-scale-v6.html, accessed 05.05.2012

Hofstede, G. (2011): Centre for Intercultural Learning, Culture does not exist, http://www.international.gc.ca/cfsi-icse/cil-cai/magazine/v02n03/1-3-eng.asp, accessed 07.04.2012

Hofstede, G., Hofstede, G.J. (n.y.): Culture, http://www.geerthofstede.eu/culture.aspx, accessed 04.04.2012

Hofstede, G., Hofstede, G.J. (n.y.): Dimensions of national Cultures, http://www.geerthofstede.nl/dimensions-of-national-cultures, accessed 24.04.2012

ITAP International (n.y.): Organizational Culture and National Culture: What's the Difference and Why does it Matter?, http://itapintl.com/whoweare/news/146-organizational-culture-and-national-culture-whats-the-difference-and-why-does-it-matter-.html?lang=, accessed 24.04.2012

Itim International (n.y.): National cultural dimensions, http://geert-hofstede.com/national-culture.html, accessed 24.04.2012

Itim International (n.y.): What about Germany, http://geert-hofstede.com/germany.html, accessed 19.05.2012

Itim International (n.y.): What about the USA, http://geert-hofstede.com/united-states.html, accessed 19.05.2012

Itim International (n.y.): Will there be one big world culture in 50 years from now?, http://geert-hofstede.com/, accessed 18.07.2012

LaBahn, W. D., Harich, K.R. (1994): Cross-National Channel Relationship Performance: The Role of Cultural Sensitivity, Conflict and Communication, accessible at: http://isbm.smeal.psu.edu/library/working-paper-articles/1994-working-papers/06-1994-cross-national-channel-relationship.pdf

Maurer, H. (n.y.): Das Prinzip des Seins, http://www.mahag.com/allg/dimens.php, accessed 17.04.2012

Oxford Dictionaries (2010): dimension, http://oxforddictionaries.com/definition/dimension?q=dimensions, accessed 17.04.2012

Pistillo, G. (2003): The Interpreter as Cultural Mediator, in: Journal of Intercultural Communication, No 6, accessible on http://www.immi.se/jicc/index.php/jicc/article/view/135/103, accessed 24.04.2012

TEIA (n.y.): Direkter und indirekter Vertrieb, http://www.teialehrbuch.de/Kostenlose-Kurse/Marketing/15336-Direkter-und-indirekter-Vertrieb.html, accessed 08.06.2012

The American Heritage Dictionary of the English Language (2003): dimension, 4th edition, accessible at http://www.thefreedictionary.com/dimension, accessed 17.04.2012

Temath, B. (n.y.): Comparing German and American Car Advertising: The Cowboy and The Engineer, http://www.tu-dortmund.de/uni/International/News/10-11-08_Car_Advertising/index.html, accessed 22.05.2012